Skin and Coat Care For Your Cat

Edited and compiled by Lowell Ackerman, DVM, PhD
Diplomate, American College of Veterinary Dermatology

TS-250

Distributed in the UNITED STATES to the Pet Trade by T.F.H. Publications, Inc., One T.F.H. Plaza, Neptune City, NJ 07753; distributed in the UNITED STATES to the Bookstore and Library Trade by National Book Network, Inc. 4720 Boston Way, Lanham MD 20706; in CANADA to the Pet Trade by H & L Pet Supplies Inc., 27 Kingston Crescent, Kitchener, Ontario N2B 2T6; Rolf C. Hagen Inc., 3225 Sartelon St. Laurent-Montreal Quebec H4R 1E8; in CANADA to the Book Trade by Vanwell Publishing Ltd., 1 Northrup Crescent, St. Catharines, Ontario L2M 6P5 ; in ENGLAND by T.F.H. Publications, PO Box 15, Waterlooville PO7 6BQ; in AUSTRALIA AND THE SOUTH PACIFIC by T.F.H. (Australia), Pty. Ltd., Box 149, Brookvale 2100 N.S.W., Australia; in NEW ZEALAND by Brooklands Aquarium Ltd. 5 McGiven Drive, New Plymouth, RD1 New Zealand; in Japan by T.F.H. Publications, Japan—Jiro Tsuda, 10-12-3 Ohjidai, Sakura, Chiba 285, Japan; in SOUTH AFRICA by Lopis (Pty) Ltd., P.O. Box 39127, Booysens, 2016, Johannesburg, South Africa. Published by T.F.H. Publications, Inc.

MANUFACTURED IN THE
UNITED STATES OF AMERICA
BY T.F.H. PUBLICATIONS, INC.

Contents

About the Editor

Lowell Ackerman, DVM, PhD, is a board-certified veterinary dermatologist and a consultant in the fields of dermatology and nutrition. He is the author of 34 books and over 150 articles and book chapters. Dr. Ackerman has lectured extensively on an international basis, including the United States, Canada, Europe and South Africa.

Preface

Skin problems represent a large proportion of veterinary visits. They are also some of the most frustrating cases to diagnose and treat. However, help is on the way! Over the past 20 years, veterinary dermatology has emerged as a major veterinary specialty and breakthroughs are being made on a regular basis. Because we now understand skin diseases much better, diagnoses are being made more routinely, and therapies are often very specific in their actions.

With all the new developments in veterinary dermatology, it is becoming exceedingly difficult for veterinarians to remain current. Fortunately, the American College of Veterinary Dermatology certifies new diplomates each year to help meet this challenge. Veterinary dermatologists work with general veterinary practitioners in a team approach to best manage stubborn skin problems. There are now dermatology specialists available in most geographic areas and a list of current board-certified dermatologists can be found in the chapter "Where to Find Help!"

The goal of this book is straightforward—to provide individuals with information about the most common skin ailments and for that information to be relayed by internationally renowned experts. All of the chapters on skin problems have been written by board-certified veterinary dermatologists. The chapter entitled "Lumps and Bumps" was written by

While they remain frustrating for both cats and owners, feline skin problems today are better diagnosed and treated than in the past years. Singapura photographed by Isabelle Francais.

a board-certified veterinary oncologist, a cancer specialist. Finally, the chapter on grooming and maintenance was written by a highly qualified professional groomer.

My thanks to all the contributors. They have done a remarkable job in distilling the important aspects of dermatologic conditions into a very readable and informative text.

Lowell Ackerman, DVM, PhD

Diplomate, American College of Veterinary Dermatology

This Scottish Fold receives regular, thorough grooming, which is reflected in the overall quality of its fur. Photo by Isabelle Francais.

Introduction

By Lowell Ackerman, DVM, PhD
Diplomate, American College of Veterinary Dermatology
Mesa Veterinary Hospital, Ltd.
858 N. Country Club Drive
Mesa, Arizona

The skin is the largest organ of the body and serves many functions, including protection from the environment, heat regulation and water balance. It accomplishes these important functions in a variety of ways. The dead surface covering of the skin (the stratum corneum) is composed of shingle-like skin cells known as keratinocytes. These cells migrate upward from deeper skin layers, eventually dying to fulfill their destiny. This whole layer (the epidermis) has no blood supply of its own; it depends on the deeper fibrous layer (the dermis) for all its nutritive needs. And, below the dermis is the subcutis, a collection of fat that provides a cushioning effect to the wear and tear of everyday life.

The haircoat (more correctly termed *fur*) is a joint project of the dermis and epidermis. Specialized cells of the epidermis extend down into the dermis, where they meet with the dermal papilla and a blood supply to form a hair follicle. After birth, no new hair follicles are produced. There are two main types of hair: the long bristly guard hairs and the downy vellus hairs. Whiskers (vibrissae) are specialized sensory hairs that have an elaborate blood and nerve supply.

But, the skin is much more than just epidermis and hair follicles. It is also an important immunologic defense mechanism that helps ward off microorganisms (bacteria, parasites, fungi) and produces antibodies against many other invaders, especially viruses. In fact, the skin immunologic system (SIS) is one of the most important defenses we have against many life-threatening infections.

Because the skin and its protective mechanisms are so complex and far-reaching, accurate diagnosis and proper management of skin problems is not always straightforward.

Karla Addington-Smith is a Certified Master Groomer from Cincinnati, Ohio. She has spent 18 years in the world of professional dog grooming. Karla is an international contest judge, grooming contest winner, noted speaker and writer. After a two-year veterinary technician program and then apprentice position, Karla opened the first of a chain of three grooming/retail shops in 1978. Karla was a member of both the 1988 and 1989 Groom Team USA and the winner of the 1988 creative grooming competition and the 1989 national groomer title at Intergroom. Karla has also collected three Cardinal Crystal Achievement Awards for the 1988 American Groomer of the Year, the 1990 Congeniality Award and the 1991 Grooming Journalist of the Year. She is well versed in business relations as well, being named the 1988 Outstanding Young Entrepreneur in America by the United States Association of Small Business and Entrepreneurship. Karla writes for various publications and is a regular contributor to Today's Breeder, Groomer to Groomer and Pet Product News magazines. She was the grooming columnist and regular feature writer for Pets Supplies Marketing magazine from 1989-1992. Karla has appeared on numerous television programs promoting pet care and education, both local and nationally. Karla now works as an independent manufacturer's representative in the pet industry as she continues to write, speak and judge.

Grooming Techniques

By Karla Addington-Smith
1358 Avalon Drive
Maineville, Ohio 45039

INTRODUCTION

Cats outnumber dogs by millions, making them America's most popular furry pet. But felines represent only a small portion of the professional groomer's clientele. Like their canine cousins, cats suffer from shedding, dry skin and flea-bite dermatitis. In addition, cats can develop stud tail and feline acne. These coat and skin problems can be relieved, or at least lessened, by regular visits to the professional groomer. Matting can be a painful problem for medium to longhaired breeds and a cause of skin irritation. Professional grooming services have direct impact on the health, comfort and well being of the feline. There is great growth potential in this virtually untapped market of catering to cats.

Grooming cats requires additional skills to safely and properly care for them even though the grooming procedure is simplified. Your efforts are concentrated on the maintenance aspect of grooming, which includes brushing, combing, nail trimming, ear cleaning, coat and skin care. The artistry is in enhancing the condition of the coat, bringing out the cat's natural beauty, not in modifying the length or style of the hair.

HANDLING

The biggest difference between working on cats and dogs is not the actual grooming process but in handling the cat's generally unpredictable nature. Reading and correctly responding to expression and body language is difficult, since most cats give little or no warning prior to biting or scratching. Handling cats takes experience and is best done by a calm

Holding the cat in the grooming assistant's lap makes for easy access to the cat's stomach and chest.

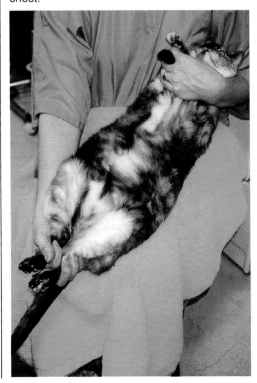

The groomer has more control over the cat's movements if the animal is held between the elbow and the body.

if necessary clips mats. The buddy system works well, especially on Cujo kitty, when restraining becomes the most difficult part of the task. The grooming assistant lays the cat on his or her lap, gently holding its front and rear legs. Hard to reach areas can be exposed for easy access and can be quickly brushed, combed or clipped.

Transporting a cat from table to tub or crate is easily done by holding the cat gently by the scruff of the neck while securing the cat between your body and opposite arm. The free hand holds the cat's front legs down and away from its body to prevent the cat from scratching you. Your bent elbow will inhibit unexpected movements

person who is prepared to react quickly to a sudden turn in behavior. A cat can not be intimidated into cooperating but will react more favorably to an individual who displays gentle but firm control.

Working on cats in a quiet area and out of sight of canines will provide a less stressful environment. The less stimulation the cat receives the more relaxed it and the groomer will be. Many professional groomers who cater to cats set aside specific hours or days for their feline clientele.

Cat grooming requires confidence and the ability to work quickly. Working in pairs is easiest. One person holds the cat as the other strategically brushes and

Instead of a grooming noose, always use a harness to restrain a cat during a grooming session.

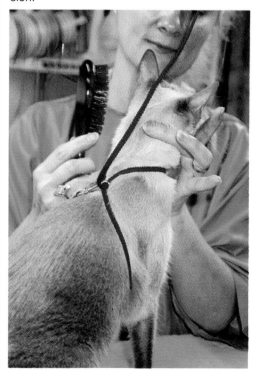

by the cat.

Quick response is needed when a feline becomes threatening. Lift the cat by the scruff of the neck and hold it at arm's length. Your free hand can grasp the hind legs to help immobilize the frisky feline until it can be safely placed in a holding crate.

If the thought of grooming a mountain lion in a Siamese cat's body brings chills to your spine, you're not alone. But practice and a few precautions can make purrfect!

PRECAUTIONS

If working alone, it is necessary to restrain the cat so you can work in confidence that it cannot bite you or escape. A harness used in

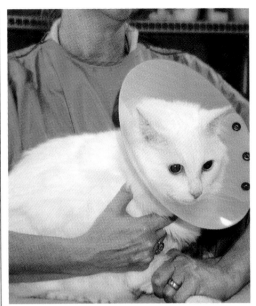

An Elizabethan collar can provide some protection against bites.

A cone-type nylon muzzle protects against bites and limits the cat's visibility, which calms the cat.

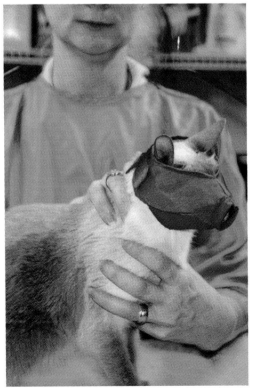

place of a grooming noose is the safest way to control the cat's movements and prevent the cat from jumping or falling from the grooming table. A towel on the grooming surface will give the cat something to sink his claws into while you work.

It is helpful to have a cage or wire basket that opens from the top in close proximity for quickly containing the problem kitty. An assortment of muzzles is a must have. Nylon cone types work well for narrow-faced cats, and Italian basket muzzles cover the entire head of short-nosed breeds. Elizabethan collars, purchased or homemade from plastic milk cartons, can offer some protection as well. Suede electrician's gloves and a long-handled fisherman's net are helpful in safely capturing a kitty on the run. A grooming noose and a looped end restraining pole are not recommended for cats, since injury can easily occur when the cat is restrained around the neck.

The proper restraining equipment is pertinent in effectively handling occasional problems that arise when working on cats, especially if you work alone. Even though most cats will never need what may sound like such extreme measures, it is best to be prepared just in case you find yourself matching strengths and wits with a house panther.

HEALTH BENEFITS

The importance of routine grooming should be stressed to the cat-owning public. Just like dogs, cats need regular grooming attention to feel and look their best. Grooming is the opportune time to check the cat for potential health problems, like teeth and ear disorders, external parasites, growths, skin diseases, irritations, clogged anal sacs etc. Thorough brushing can reduce or eliminate hairball problems as well.

A kitten should be exposed to the brushing, combing, bathing process early in its young life. Beginning then will help to desensitize the kitten to the handling and hustle bustle of the grooming shop as grooming becomes an enjoyable, if not tolerated, part of its life.

PRELIMINARIES

Before the actual grooming process begins, you will need to take a step of precaution to protect yourself from scratches. The cat's nails will need to be cut with a sharp cat claw trimmer. These trimmers move in a scissor fashion and are especially designed to accommodate the fragile, rather flat-sided nail of the cat. Have styptic powder on hand in case a nail is clipped too short.

Additional protection can be obtained by using veterinary non-adhesive wrap on the cat's feet to cover the claws. Do not use adhesive-type bandages. Removal of such a product can pull hair and leave sticky residue on the coat.

Once equipment has been gathered and nails have been trimmed, you can begin the grooming procedure. Clean the cat's ears with a mild ear cleanser. Inspect the ears for mites, infection or other irritations. Report your findings to the client and recommend veterinary attention when necessary.

Short-nosed breeds have a tendency to develop staining under the eyes, which can be swabbed with a tear stain remover that is safe for cats. Staining can be temporarily lightened by applying corn starch to the area. The folds in the face of short-nosed breeds can be cleaned with a cotton swab and lightly dusted with corn starch to help keep them dry.

Stud tail is a concentrated patch of oil glands located on the top of the tail just up from the base. An oily secretion causes the unsightly dark spot and contrary to what the name implies, the condition affects both males and females. If the cat is not getting bathed, use grooming powder or corn starch to absorb the oil and lighten the spot. A grease-cutting detergent used

Non-adhesive veterinary wrap protects the groomer from scratches.

ness or hair loss in this area to the owner and recommend veterinary attention when needed. These oil glands are susceptible to becoming clogged and secondary infections can easily occur. Specialized prescription medications are required in advanced or chronic cases.

BRUSHING TECHNIQUES

As with the canine, brushing is a fundamental part of caring for the cat. Shedding can be minimized by regular brushing as the bristles grasp the loose hair and remove it before hair sticks to carpet and furniture and more importantly before the cat swallows it, causing potential problems with hairballs. Brushing is pertinent to the overall health and comfort of the cat and is a good time to look for external parasites as you work your way through the coat.

Short-coated breeds will require a natural bristle brush used against, then with the growth of the hair. This process will loosen and remove dead hair and skin as it distributes natural oils throughout the coat. A rubber brush used lightly will loosen and remove dead hair and polish the coat. Finish off the grooming by rubbing a chamois or velvet with the growth of hair to bring out the natural shine and remove any loose hair, dust or dander.

Medium-haired coats will benefit from a gentle variety slicker brush used by lifting the coat and brushing from the skin out. Use your fingers to gently pull small tangles or mats apart that you

only on this area is a safe and effective way of removing the excess oils and dirt during the bath. Stud tail should be looked at closely to determine if the sebaceous glands have become infected. Look for hair loss, inflammation, swelling and bumps. Veterinary attention is needed whenever the area is inflamed or infected.

Feline acne is a crusty scale that can develop on a cat's chin and is also caused by a concentrated patch of oil glands. Using your fingernail or flea comb, gently remove the dry crust, and cleanse the area with isopropyl alcohol, medicated acne pads, or a grease-cutting medicated shampoo. Again, report any swelling, red-

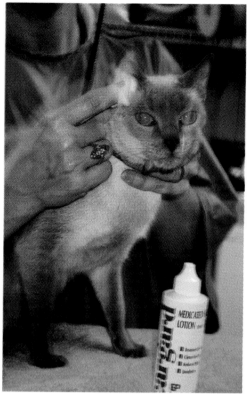

Use a gentle cleansing agent formulated for cats to swab the ears.

may find in the rough of the neck, rump and tail area. A seam ripper, found in fabric and crafts stores, can be used to separate small, tight mats. A regular mat comb is not advisable for cats as their skin is far too fragile. After the coat has been brushed thoroughly using the layering technique, test what you have brushed with a Greyhound style comb. This metal comb has narrow teeth that easily penetrate the coat, finding tiny mats that may lie against the skin. Be sure to insert the comb parallel to the skin to avoid causing undo discomfort or irritation.

Long-haired cats require the same line brushing technique with a gentle variety slicker brush. Pay special attention to the chest, behind the ears, underbelly and under legs. These are friction points that quickly become severely matted if ignored. Be sure to check the coat with a Greyhound style comb.

It must be mentioned that a cat's skin is extremely thin and sensitive. It is important that the grooming tools be used with care and a gentle touch to prevent irritation, tearing or damage.

CLIPPING

Long-haired cats make such adorable kittens. What begins as a handful of fluff quickly becomes a hair-growing machine that needs lots of brushing attention to stay attractive and healthy. Many people unwittingly take these adorable kitties home, only to find the care of their coats overwhelming. So, due to ignorance, neglect or customer choice, it is common but not always pretty, that these cats are clipped short.

Many times the groomer has no choice; the cat is simply in such poor shape that it must be shaved. If this is the case, then rarely will you need to clip shorter than the #10 or #15 blade. Find an opening in the matting and begin by clipping with the grain. Normally the pelted coat will have some new growth underneath that will allow the blade to slide between the skin and matted hair with general ease. Pay special attention to the temperature of the blade. A blade cooling lubricant used frequently will lessen the chance of burning the cat's sensitive skin. Use gentle pressure and pull the skin taut as you clip. Longer hair can be left around the head and on the tail if possible so that the cat has some style. The feline, in all its dignity, will certainly find this less humiliating!

I shared my life with a Turkish Angora for 17 years. She was raised with grooming and behaved better for her quarterly clipping than many of my canine clients. Nuisance and I both hated her long hair, I because it was all over my gray carpeting and she because of the nasty hairballs she would develop. So began the ritual of clipping her short into the Lion Trim. We were both happier with each other. Cat fanciers would argue against this for aesthetics and the fact that clipping the guard hairs does change the texture of the coat. But clipping is an option that can benefit both cat and owner. I am of the opinion that a cat is better off clipped short for comfort reasons then left ungroomed to suffer in neglect.

Medium-haired cats can have profuse coat around their neck, rump and tail. These areas are problem spots and need regular attention. It is not uncommon for these areas to need clipping if the matting has gotten bad. Usually isolating the mat and shaving it out will not be too noticeable as the longer hair will cover the holes in the coat.

A cat left ungroomed can be a

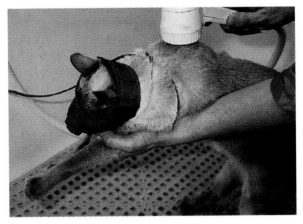

Hold the spray nozzle against the skin to wet the coat quickly and prevent frightening the cat with spraying water.

real challenge. Accustomed to little handling, the matted cat may reject any attempt at grooming it. The professional groomer will need to make a decision as to what extent he or she will go to complete the grooming process. If the cat becomes a danger to you or itself, it is acceptable that you recommend the cat be sedated and handled at the veterinarian's office.

BATHING

Cats in general are fastidious self groomers. It is quite possible that with little more than regular brushing many cats would never need to be bathed. Bathing becomes necessary when the cat is soiled, develops a skin condition requiring medicated treatments or when combatting an external parasite problem.

The cat should be restrained in the tub by a harness, and a screen or towel placed in the bottom of the tub will help the cat feel more secure. On occasion, a muzzle may be necessary to limit the cat's visibility. This usually has a calming effect on the cat. A nylon cat bag can be used to limit its mobility while bathing.

Place cotton in each ear to prevent water from entering the canal. Check the water temperature. To avoid frightening the cat with spraying water, hold the spray nozzle against the cat's skin, allowing the water to penetrate the coat quickly. Apply the appropriate shampoo according to directions and lather well. Rinse. Repeat the process if necessary.

It is very important that only products labeled safe for cats should be used on cats. This is especially important when using flea and tick remedies. Gently squeeze off excess water and wrap the cat in a clean dry towel. Towel dry until just damp. Brush through the damp coat to break up clumps of hair. Cage drying can be used with care. Be sure the cage is well ventilated and contains a floor grate to allow air flow underneath the cat.

High-velocity drying should be avoided. Not only does the sound and force of the air flow cause panic in even the most mild-mannered cats, the breathing of water particles is a health hazard to the respiratory problem-prone feline. The best finish will be achieved by fluff drying. The gentle flow of warm air is relaxing to most cats, whose owners will appreciate the fluffy and glossy finish this procedure brings out in the coat.

For cats that tolerate all aspects of grooming except bathing, dry shampoo or cleansing powders are a viable alternative. Work the product into the coat and use a bristle brush and fluff drying technique to remove the powder from the coat. Wear a dust mask and blow the powder away from the cat as you work.

SUMMARY

Professional cat grooming is a valuable service to the cat-owning public. Brushing up on your feline handling and grooming skills is a necessary prerequisite. However, with a small investment in some specialized cat grooming products and handling equipment, you can be the cat's meow when it comes to caring for and about felines!

Equipment and products formulated for use on cats make the grooming process safer and more effective.

Additional Reading

T.F.H. Publications offers a wide selection of general and specialized cat books, available at pet shops everywhere.

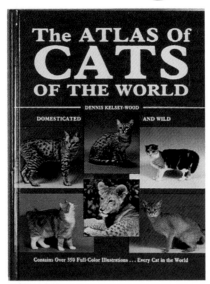

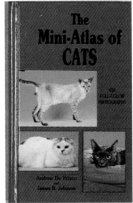

TS-152
THE MINI-ATLAS OF CATS
480 pages
nearly 500 full-color photos

TS-127
THE ATLAS OF CATS OF THE WORLD
300 pages
over 350 full-color photos

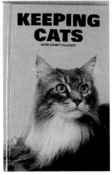

TS-219
KEEPING CATS
192 pages
80 full-color photos

TW-103
THE PROPER CARE OF CATS
256 pages
258 full-color photos

TS-173
THE ALLURE OF THE CAT
304 pages
420 full-color photos

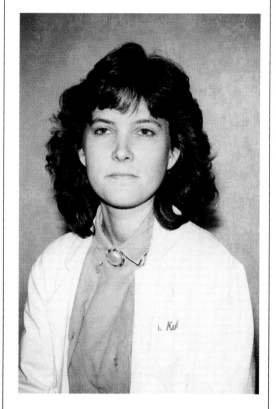

Karen Kuhl received her Doctor of Veterinary Medicine from the University of Illinois in 1987. She was a primary care veterinarian in the Detroit area for two years prior to completing a residency in comparative dermatology at the University of Pennsylvania. She is now a board-certified veterinary dermatologist and is currently practicing veterinary dermatology in Downers Grove, Illinois.

Fleas and Ticks

By Karen A. Kuhl, DVM
Diplomate, American College of Veterinary Dermatology
Animal Allergy and Dermatology
2551 Warrenville Rd.
Downers Grove,, IL 60515

INTRODUCTION

It is essential to understand the life cycle of the flea to have appropriate flea control, since many of the insecticides are effective against different developmental stages of the flea. The types of insecticides available will be discussed. Unless otherwise specified, the products discussed should be available from veterinarians or pet stores. It is very important to read and understand ingredients since new flea and tick products are developed often. Additionally, the forms in which the products can be applied will be discussed.

LIFE CYCLE OF THE FLEA

Although numerous species of fleas are known, the primary flea to infest both dogs and cats is the cat flea, *Ctenocephalides felis*. Flea eggs are the size of a grain of sand. They are laid on the cat, but are not sticky and immediately fall onto the ground. The flea eggs then hatch into larvae in 1-10 days. All stages of the flea life cycle are very temperature and humidity dependent. Humidity of 50% or less will desiccate (dry out) the eggs. That's why flea problems are at their worst in warm and humid environments.

The flea eggs hatch into larvae that are yellow and approximately 2 mm long. These larvae are free living and primarily feed on the fecal material produced by adult fleas. As they ingest the adult feces, the larvae become darker in color. Larvae dislike light so they try to bury themselves deep in carpet fibers or soil or under grass and branches outside. The larval stage lasts about 5-11 days. Temperatures below 65-70°F and humidity below 70% prolong their development. After this stage, the larva spins a silk-like cocoon in which it pupates.

The cocoon is whitish and about $^1/_4$ long. It is sticky and often becomes coated with debris from the environment which makes it difficult to see. The pupal stage usually lasts 8-9 days but may last up to 174 days. This tends to be the stage which most resists flea control. The pupae are stimulated to emerge from the cocoon to become

Ctenocephalides felis, the cat flea...Closer than you'd ever want it to be.

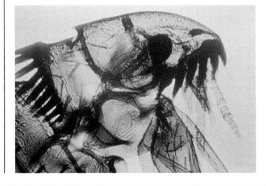

adult fleas by heat, vibrations and exhaled breath (carbon dioxide).

Under average environmental conditions, the flea life cycle takes 3-4 weeks, but can take as long as 6 months. Upon emergence from the cocoon, the adult fleas are attracted to pets by the warmth of the animal's body, movement, changes in light intensity and exhaled carbon dioxide. The newly emerged fleas are found in the carpet, and at this stage most often bite humans prior to finding a suitable host.

For many years, veterinarians were taught that adult fleas spend little time on pets and reside primarily in the environment. Recent research suggests that the cat flea resides on the cat or dog almost continuously since it requires a constant blood source. The cat flea can only survive 10-14 days without a blood meal and cannot mate until it has acquired its first blood meal; it mates within 12 hours of feeding. Egg production begins within 48 hours of the first blood meal. Female cat fleas may produce over 2,000 eggs during their lifetime. Only a fraction develop to adult fleas, but this method of reproduction does explain why fleas have existed for so long. The higher the temperature and lower the humidity the quicker fleas will die. Temperatures of 68-72°F and humidity greater than 60% are the most ideal conditions for fleas. Fleas are unable to survive temperatures below 40°F for 10 or more days.

When people arrive in a home that is previously uninhabited for some time and are promptly bitten by a number of fleas, it is usually due to adult fleas emerging from the pupal stages found in carpets. An alternative is that the attic, basement or crawl spaces are inhabited by raccoons, opossums or stray cats that are infested with fleas. Squirrels, rabbits and birds are rarely infested with the cat flea.

Flea larvae. These are the forms that live in the environment but can't yet bite.

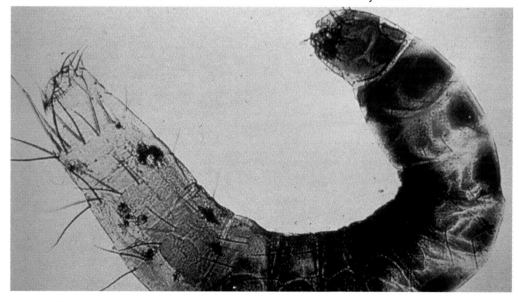

Rhipacephalus sanguineus tick. Photo courtesy of Allerderm/Virbac.

LIFE CYCLE OF TICKS

Ticks are very important due to the large number of diseases they are capable of transmitting to man and animals. They can cause life-threatening anemias and paralysis and a host of other diseases. Two main families of ticks exist–soft shell and hard shell. This discussion will be limited primarily to the hard shell variety. The most common ticks seen in small animals are *Rhipicephalus sanguineus*, *Dermacentor* species, *Ixodes*, and some species of *Amblyomma*. Their entire life cycle can take 2-3 years and they may survive for long periods of time without food. The adults lay one large batch of eggs which hatch in 1-4 weeks and then enter a resting period prior to molting to the nymph stage. The nymph feeds, rests and then molts to an adult.

THE SIGNS OF FLEA BITE HYPERSENSITIVITY

Flea bite hypersensitivity is due to an allergic reaction to substances contained in flea saliva. Flea saliva is deposited in a cat's skin when a flea bites. An allergic cat may react minutes to several days after a bite occurs.

Cats with flea bite hypersensitivity tend to be extremely itchy. They frantically chew at the base of their tails, their flanks/thighs, and groin. They may also scratch around their necks, ears and sides.

The scratching and nibbling may become generalized. When the scratching and chewing is moderate to severe, cats may develop alopecia (hair loss), and hyperpigmentation (dark discoloration of the skin) on their backs, tailbase, groin and inner thighs. Cats may also develop numerous tiny crusts (scabs) on their backs (feline miliary dermatitis). This may be associated with a number of diseases, but most commonly flea bite allergy. Occasionally, these cats scratch and bite everywhere. Other signs seen with flea bite allergy are bald stomachs, symmetrical hair loss with no crusts and firm, raised ulcerated plaques (eosinophilic plaques). Tapeworms, spread by fleas, are another sign that fleas are present.

These cats tend to have fewer fleas than flea-infested cats. This often surprises owners because they expect their cat to have lots of fleas if they are, in fact, allergic. The apparent lack of fleas may be due to the constant chewing and mechanical removal of the fleas or the cat's allergic reaction may actually adversely impact on the number of fleas. Consequently, the fleas are often very difficult to find, and the diagnosis may be based on clinical signs and response to appropriate flea control therapy.

Flea infestation differs from flea bite hypersensitivity in that there are usually many fleas evident on the cat. Both cat and environment tend to contain large numbers of fleas in various stages of development. These cats may or may not exhibit the clini-

Dermacentor variabilis tick. Photo courtesy Allerderm/Virbac.

Egg-laying *Dermacentor* tick. Photo courtesy Allerderm/Virbac.

cal signs discussed above. The fact is that the cats that have the most fleas are least likely to be allergic.

TICK PROBLEMS

Ticks congregate predominantly in the ears, between the toes and around the head and neck. If ticks are found, the tick should be soaked in alcohol to loosen its hold on the animal. Then the tick should be grasped (with a gloved hand or tick-removing forceps) close to the point of attachment and removed with gradual pressure. Be careful to remove all mouthparts. If some mouthparts remain, the cat may develop a secondary bacterial infection. Unless paralyzed or otherwise debilitated, the animal should then be sprayed or dipped completely to kill any remaining ticks that may have been overlooked.

FLEA AND TICK CONTROL

Flea and tick control and prevention are important. Flea control and prevention consist of a multi-pronge attack. The flea allergic animal must have not only the adult fleas on him/her killed, but also should have a repellant applied to prevent any additional fleas in the area from biting. Additionally, environmental control MUST be performed. It is essential that house treatment be done in cases of flea and tick infestation. Yard treatment is also important in most areas of the country.

Insecticides That Work the Best

The safest insecticides available are pyrethrins and pyrethroids. Pyrethrins are derived from chrysanthemums and pyrethroids are their synthetic derivatives. Pyrethrin kills fleas quickly but needs to be used with a potentiator (synergist) to achieve maximum effect. Pyrethrins are also rapidly degraded by sunlight. Their activity can be enhanced by a process called microencapsulation, in which the pyrethrins are enclosed in little beads which only release their contents slowly. No evidence of resistance to this substance has been noted. Permethrin (a pyrethroid) has relatively low toxicity if used according to label directions. It is more stable than natural pyrethrin in the presence of sunlight and does not need to be used with potentiating chemicals (synergists). It may stick to nylon carpet fibers, which can reduce its effectiveness. Pure permethrin sprays are not approved for use on cats.

Organophosphates and carbamates are the most effective insecticides but are also more toxic than pyrethrins and pyrethroids. Chlorpyrifos, an organophosphate, is extensively used in commercial products and by professional exterminators and works well against fleas. It is also available in microencapsulated form (bound into little beads that slowly release their contents into the environment) for good residual effect. Chlorpyrifos should NOT be applied directly on cats although it can be used in the environment. When using organophosphates, follow label directions precisely. These chemicals may have cumulative toxic effects resulting in neurologic signs. Immediate side effects include constricted pupils, tearing, vomiting, diarrhea, drooling, frequent urination, difficulty

Ixodes dammini, the tick that causes Lyme disease. Photo courtesy of Allerderm/Virbac.

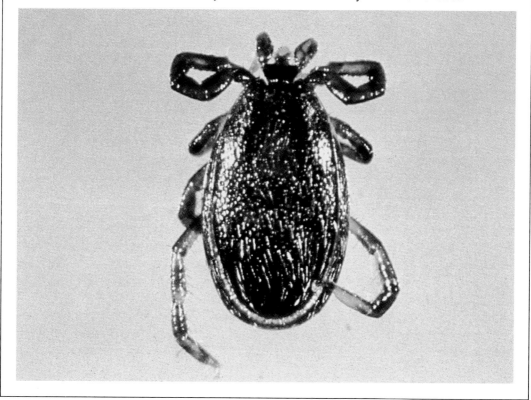

breathing, slow heart rate and low blood pressure. Organophosphates should not be used on cats, older sick animals or very young animals. If used properly and under veterinary supervision, these products are very effective for good environmental flea control.

Malathion is another commonly used environmental organophosphate. This is very effective against fleas and has relatively low toxicity. It should not be used with other organophosphates. Owners commonly make the mistake of using organophosphates in dips, as collars, and indoor and outdoor sprays; the cumulative effect can overwhelm a cat (and other family members) and can have lethal consequences. Diazinon, another environmental organophosphate, has a long residual effect and insects do not easily become resistant to it. This is also available in a microencapsulated form. Again, do not use this with other organophosphates; minimize the exposure of cats to all organophosphates.

Carbamates such as carbaryl may also be applied to the yard. Carbaryl (e.g., Sevin™) is a carbamate that is often used as a pesticide for crops. The literature suggests this may not work as well in the southeastern United States as it does in other areas. Toxicity is low, but fleas and ticks often become resistant to this insecticide. Carbaryl, diazinon and malathion can be obtained from yard care stores.

Insect Growth Regulators (IGRs) are not insecticides but they do have a valuable role in flea control. Methoprene and pyripoxyfen mimic natural insect growth regulators and are extremely safe and almost entirely non-toxic. Insect growth regulators are natural control substances; they are present in the environment in large amounts during the larval stage of development, but must decrease for the flea to enter the pupal stage. If methoprene and pyripoxyfen levels are high in the environment (because you used an IGR-containing flea control product), the larvae can not pupate and will eventually die. Both substances also kill eggs but do not affect adult fleas. Beneficial effects of this type of product will not be seen for 1-4 weeks indoors (because they don't actually kill the adult fleas you can see). These two substances are usually used in conjunction with synergized pyrethrins (immediate kill) and/or an organophosphate (chlorpyrifos for extended activity) in the environment. Unfortunately, methoprene is broken down by sunlight and loses its effectiveness and therefore is not useful outdoors. Fenoxycarb can be used outdoors since it is light stable but has recently been recalled by the manufacturer. The insect growth regulators are an important part of good flea control.

Sodium polyborate is an inert substance (borax) that is used for flea control when applied to carpets. This is an effective and safe means of flea control. The fleas are literally desiccated (dried out) by this substance. It is available through local distributors whose numbers can be obtained from veterinarians.

Synergists are also not insecticides but they help insecticides work better. The two most common synergists are piperonyl butoxide and N-octyl bicycloheptene dicarb-oximide. Synergists are safe and allow a higher level of killing by safer agents such as the pyrethrins. Piperonyl butoxide should not be used in concentrations greater than 1.0% in cats since it may cause tremors, lethargy and incoordination at these levels.

Repellents are chemicals that cause insects to move away. MGK326 (di-N-propyl isocinchomeronate), butoxypolypropylene glycol and DEET are examples. Pyrethrins and permethrins both have repellant activity. Most repellants have toxic potential in cats and should be used cautiously and strictly according to manufacturer's recommendations.

Treating the Indoor Environment

A vacuum with a beater bar can remove between 15-20% of the larvae and 32-59% of eggs in the carpet. Therefore, vacuuming should be done prior to application of any insecticides. This will also allow more effective usage of any parasiticide products since the carpet fibers will be raised. The vacuum bag should immediately be taped and removed from the premises so any immature stages of the fleas do not further develop in your home. Other cleaning measures are also worthwhile. The pet's bedding should be washed at least weekly and dried on a high heat setting.

There are several types of insec-

ticides available for application in the house. They primarily consist of permethrin, chlorpyrifos, microen-capsulated chlorpyrifos, Insect Growth Regulators (methoprene and fenoxycarb), synergized pyrethrins and sodium polyborate. Examples are Duratrol™ (microencapsulated chlorpyrifos), Sectrol™ (microencapsulated synergized pyrethrins), Ectoguard™ (synergized pyrethrin and fenoxycarb) and Ultraban™ (chlorpyrifos and fenoxycarb).

Flea control in the house differs somewhat in different areas of the country. In general, extermination by a professional exterminator tends to be somewhat more expensive, but much less labor intensive. The professional exterminator does have access to some chemicals that are unavailable to veterinarians or consumers if an especially severe flea infestation is present. Application of the insecticides by the owner can be accomplished through the use of total-release aerosols or foggers. Aerosols are most easily applied with compressed air sprayers. These need to be applied after vacuuming to the surface of all rugs, carpets, baseboards and upholstered furniture. They should always be tested on an inconspicuous area to determine color fastness of fabric. In the author's opinion, application with a compressed air sprayer is much more effective than foggers. The foggers do not penetrate along baseboards or under furniture nearly as well. If foggers are used, a a separate can of fogger should be used for each of the rooms. Follow the label directions for area size. Follow-up should be done with a sprayer in inaccessible areas. Do not expect one application to remedy the problem. Most insecticide sprays need to be re-applied in 2-4 weeks, and Insect Growth Regulators last about 2-3 months.

Typical commercially available products are applied twice, times two weeks apart after vacuuming, and then monthly. The second application after 2 weeks is recommended due to the continued emergence of adult fleas from the cocoons which are resistant to most environmental treatments. Again, recommendations differ according to the area of the country. It is very important to seek the opinion of your primary care veterinarian or veterinary dermatologist on application frequency for your particular area of the country.

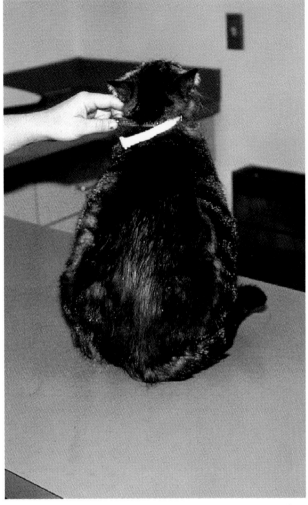

Typical area of hair loss seen with flea infestations and flea-bite hypersensitivity.

CONTROLLING FLEAS OUTDOORS

It is important to remember that fleas and ticks will thrive in areas protected from the direct sunlight and where the soil is moist. Therefore, removing any organic debris and brush under bushes and mowing and raking the yard will help. Keep the garage and areas under porches as clean as possible. Entrances to crawl spaces, attics and garages should be sealed. Finally, when applying flea and tick treatments, do the shaded and shel-

tered areas primarily. Fleas and their offspring tend to inhabit the well lit and sun-exposed areas less frequently.

The most commonly used chemicals outdoors are chlorpyrifos (Dursban™), microencapsulated chlorpyrifos, growth inhibitors, malathion, diazinon and carbaryl. Be sure young children and pets do not ingest or contact the organophosphate granules after application.

For best results outside, only

light-stable products should be used. The yard and kennel preparations should not be applied to the animals. The liquids can be applied with a compressed air sprayer.

Finally, some new flea control products (Interrupt™ Veterinary Product Laboratories; Bio Flea Halt™-Biosys; Bio Safe™-Ortho) that sound very promising have recently become available. The active ingredient is a beneficial nematode (worm) called *Steinernema carpocapsae*. This nematode is naturally occurring and is a parasite of fleas in nature. This product's key features are no odor or staining, environmentally safe to pets, children and wildlife, no contamination of water supplies and high efficacy and long term effect. This flea product inhibits the pupal and larval stages and does not interact with any topicals or systemic preparations such as the organophosphates.

SAFE FLEA CONTROL ON YOUR CAT

On-animal flea control is the final prong. This begins using a flea comb (32 teeth/inch) daily in short-haired cats or kittens. Flea combs are very effective but are under-utilized by the public. This non-toxic method of flea control should be part of everyone's approach to a flea-free pet. The material collected using a flea comb can be examined for evidence of fleas and flea feces.

Flea shampoos do kill fleas on contact but give the owner a false sense of security. It must be remembered that there is NO long term effect with a flea shampoo as it is all rinsed off. Therefore, a dip or flea spray will still have to be applied. Shampoos (pyrethrin-based) are best used in kittens (be sure label-approved for kittens!) and in flea infestations. Alone, they are not effective for flea bite hypersensitivities.

Sprays are highly effective if applied correctly. The entire haircoat should be dampened. Concentrate on the base of the tail along the back, under the chin and in the groin. The head and neck should be treated first before spray is applied to the rest of the body. Do NOT spray directly into the cat's eyes. In some cats, it is best to apply the spray to a towel and then wipe this on the cat since they resent the hissing sound of sprays. Sprays containing safe insecticides combined with IGRs are good since they kill both adult fleas and eggs. Pyrethrin-synergist and repellant sprays are also good because they provide quick kill and prevent fleas from biting. Examples of pyrethrin and permethrin-containing sprays are Duocide LA™ (Virbac), Synerkyl™ (DVM), Mycodex 14 Day Spray™ (Smith Kline Beecham) and Two Way Pet Foam™ (3-M Animal Care Products). Cats tend to tolerate flea foams better than other application methods. Examples are Two Way Flea Foam™ (3M Animal Care Products) and Ectofoam™ (Virbac).

Flea collars also provide owners with a false sense of security and are not the most effective means of flea control. Therefore, they are not recommended. Electronic flea collars are also not worth the money. No independent studies done to date have found them to be effective.

Dips or sponge-ons are highly effective for killing adult fleas and provide prolonged residual activity. Always follow label directions to be sure appropriate dilutions are maintained and wear gloves when applying the dips. Organophosphate dips such as phosmet (Paramite™ Zoecon/ VetKem) and chlorpyrifos (Duratrol™ 3M Animal Care Products) should not be applied to cats. A pyrethrin and rotenone based sponge-on (Durakyl™-DVM) is approved for cats but must be used with caution, as toxic reactions have been seen. When dips are applied, they should not be rinsed off. Powders are a matter of preference. Many people do not like the dust on their animals.

Systemic flea control products effectively kill fleas. Again, the flea must first bite the animal to get its dose of flea control. This is not effective in flea allergic animals since the bite is the cause of the allergy. Systemic products are available through veterinarians. The current systemic, cythioate, (Proban™ Haver) is not licensed for use in cats. Products like fenthion (Pro-Spot™ Haver) are applied to the skin but quickly make their way to the bloodstream and must also be considered systemic agents. None are recommended for routine use in the cat. A new oral medication, lufenuron, seems to have low toxicity according to recent studies but will need to be used with other topicals in flea-

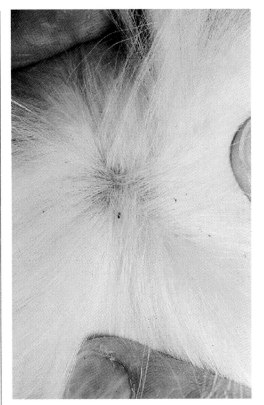

Part the fur to see evidence of fleas and flea feces.

allergic animals.

INEFFECTIVE FLEA CONTROL PRACTICES

According to scientific research, brewer's yeast, B-complex vitamins and elemental sulfur products are ineffective in repelling or killing fleas. It is therefore difficult to understand why many pet owners believe that they do work. It is also important to remember that some "natural" therapies are themselves potentially toxic and should not be considered harmless.

SUMMARY

Flea and tick control must be tailored for each situation. Most

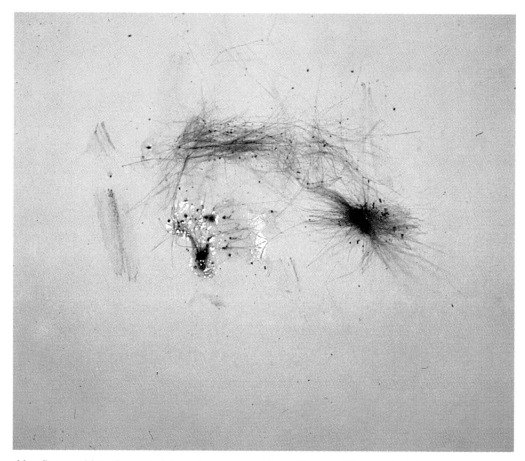

After flea combing, the material can be examined for evidence of fleas or their feces.

importantly, you must treat both the environment and the pet. Treating just one or the other will leave everyone frustrated. Remember too that safety is an important concern when it comes to flea and tick control; always use the safest products available. Finally, any questions or concerns regarding specific products should be addressed to your veterinarian or the product's manufacturer.

ADDITIONAL READING

Garris, G.I.: Control of ticks. Veterinary Clinics of North America, *Small Animal Practice*, 1991; 21(1): 173-183.

MacDonald, J.M.: Flea allergy dermatitis and flea control. In *Current Veterinary Dermatology*, Griffin, C.E.; Kwochka, K.W.; MacDonald, J.M. (Eds.). Mosby Year Book, St. Louis, MO, 1993, pp 57-71.

Muller, G.H.; Kirk, R.W.; Scott, D.W.: *Small Animal Dermatology*, 4th Ed., W.B. Saunders Company, Philadelphia, 1989, 1007pp.

Sosna, C.G.; Medleau, L.: The clinical signs and diagnosis of external parasite infestation. *Veterinary Medicine*, 1992; 87: 549-564.

A regular grooming regimen is important, especially for longhaired cats. Birman photographed by Isabelle Francais.

Dr. Thomas P. Lewis II received his veterinary degree from Colorado State University in 1986. After a two-year practice internship, he entered an approved residency in dermatology in 1988; in 1991, he successfully completed the certification boards of the American College of Veterinary Dermatology. Dr. Lewis now operates animal dermatology referral practices in Arizona, New Mexico, and Utah.

Managing Mange

By Thomas P. Lewis II, DVM
Diplomate, American College of Veterinary Dermatology
Mesa Veterinary Hospital, Ltd.
858 N. Country Club Drive
Mesa, AZ 85201

INTRODUCTION

Mites are microscopic parasites related to ticks that, in general, live permanently on or in the skin of their host. They usually prefer or require to live on one specific species, and as they feed, live, and die on the animal, they cause mechanical damage to the skin. In addition they may secrete irritating substances or produce allergic reactions. Sometimes severe secondary bacterial infections of the skin are seen due to mite infestation.

CHEYLETIELLOSIS

Cheyletiellosis is commonly known as "walking dandruff" and is caused by three species: *Cheyletiella yasguri, C. blackei,* and *C. parasitovorax,* which generally affect dogs, cats, and rabbits respectively. There is some crossover between mite species and the animals they will infest. All species of *Cheyletiella* have prominent hooked-shaped mouth parts that give them a distinct appearance. All four pairs of legs extend past the body margins. These mites live on the surface of the skin where they feed on tissue fluids and debris. The life cycle requires two to three weeks to complete and is spent entirely on the animal. The mites may be spread between animals by either direct or indirect contact and the infestation is highly contagious, especially between young animals in unsanitary conditions. These mites are most highly contagious by direct contact but can potentially be spread through kennel or hospital cages or by grooming tools if they are not cleaned, dried, and sprayed with insecticides.

The diagnosis is usually made by finding either the mite or its eggs on a skin scraping. Careful inspection of the scaly skin surface with a magnifying hand lens will sometimes reveal the white mites moving around on the skin and hair. This is not a very reli-

An itchy cat afflicted with cheyletiellosis. Some cats may have minimal itching. Others will have just dandruff.

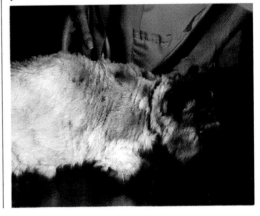

able method, however, as the mites must be actively moving in order to be seen. Skin scrapings do not have to be as deep, but multiple skin scrapings are sometimes necessary to find even one mite, as the actual number of mites may be low. Material and debris collected from the scraping is then viewed with a microscope.

The clinical signs (symptoms) in cats with cheyletiellosis will be variable. The most common initial problem is scale (dandruff) along the top of the body. Pruritus (itching) is variable, with some patients being very itchy while others are not itchy at all. Cats which have no clinical changes have been found and are called "carriers." Animals with the most severe itching actually become allergic to the mites and their by-products. It is possible for a very low number of mites to create a significant amount of itching, scale, and other changes and be difficult to find due to their low numbers. These changes are similar to allergic reactions from other causes, such as food or inhalant allergies which can make arriving at the correct diagnosis more challenging. *Cheyletiella* mites have the potential to infest humans and may result in a small red itchy rash (bumps and spots) on the arms, trunk, and buttocks. The mite cannot complete its life cycle on people and will not reproduce; however, affected individuals should seek appropriate medical care.

Cheyletiella is unusual in that the female may survive off the animal for up to 10-14 days. Therefore, successful therapy may require treatment of the environment as well as the animal. *Cheyletiella* is sensitive to most of the insecticides used for environmental flea control. Various therapies are effective for cheyletiellosis. Weekly lime sulfur dips (2-3%) have been the standard treatment, and are still effective most of the time. Complete contact with the skin (not just the top layer of the coat) is necessary but more difficult in long-coated breeds. Ivermectin has been found to be effective in both dogs and cats. The drug is not FDA-approved in cats at this dose, and unexpected reactions have been reported. Reactions are quite rare however, and ivermectin is the first drug of choice for many veterinary dermatologists when treating cheyletiellosis in cats. All animals on the premises should be treated, as asymptomatic carriers do exist and could act as a source of reinfestation. Pyrethrins and rotenone powder have also been used in cats with success, but contact with the skin is difficult to achieve with powders. Shampoos and spray formulations of these products are preferable to powders. Other types of treatment in cats include carbaryl and organophosphates, although these will have more side effects. Labels should be read closely to ensure they are safe for cats prior to usage.

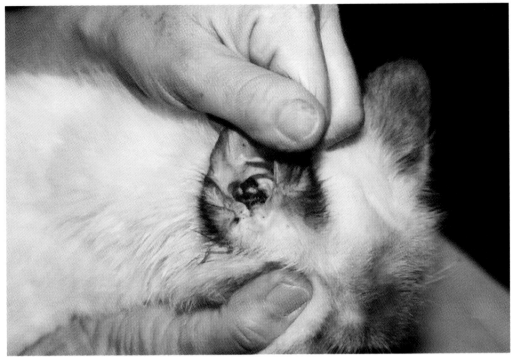

Ear mites are a common parasite of both cats and dogs.

EAR MITES (OTOACARIASIS)

Otodectic mange (ear mites) is caused by the psoroptic mite *Otodectes cynotis*. The mite lives on the surface of the skin and does not burrow and has been shown to feed on lymph and blood. The life cycle is completed on the animal. Three to four weeks are required to complete the life cycle from eggs to larva, protonymph, deutonymph and finally adult. Transmission is by direct contact, as the mite dies quickly after it has been removed from the animal.

The outer ear canal is the favorite location for *Otodectes*, but the mite has been found in other locations such as the face, neck, feet, and tailhead. Clinical signs include variable degrees of itching and head shaking. Lesions include scratched skin around the ears and the accumulation of dark brown to black "coffee grounds-like" debris in the outer ear canal. Mites create irritation and damage to the ear and skin tissue because of their direct contact with the skin. In addition to irritation, the mites can also stimulate allergic-type reactions on the skin and ears, which intensifies the damage. Some cats will carry the mite yet show no symptoms or signs. These patients have not yet developed an allergy to the mite and are called "carriers." The animals with the most severe itching actually become allergic to the mites and their by-products. It is possible for a very low number of mites to

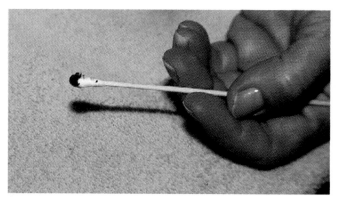

A swab taken from a pet with ear mites. Notice the dark color of the material.

and the black debris from the ear canal onto a glass slide and then viewing with a micro-scope will usually re-veal the mites if they are present. Some cats with outer ear infec-tions due to other causes such as aller-gies are mistakenly treated as recurring or "resistant" cases of ear mites. Evaluation for food allergies and inhalant (en-vironmental) allergies is indi-cated in these patients.

create a significant amount of itching, scale, and other changes, but be difficult to find due to their low numbers.

The diagnosis is definitively made by observing the mites. This may be either with the aid of an otoscope or microscope. Mixing a small amount of mineral oil

Treatment includes cleaning or flushing the ear canal to remove all debris and then instilling miti-cidal (mite-killing) agents such as rotenone or thiabendazole topically into the ear. In addi-

Microscopic view of the ear mite *Otodectes cynotis*.

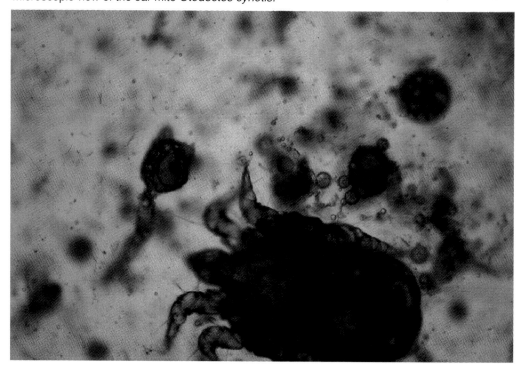

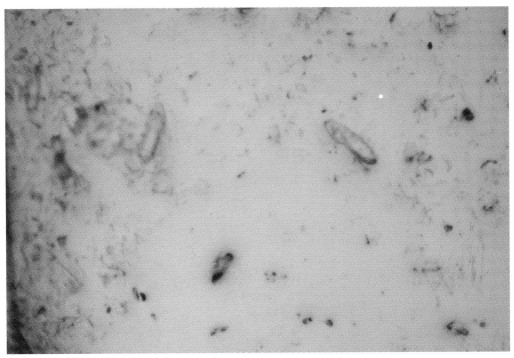

Microscopic view of the *Demodex cati* mite.

tion, the rest of the animal should be lightly treated with a flea powder or spray to kill any mites outside of the ear canal. Most products which kill the adult mites will not kill the eggs. One single treatment will therefore not result in a cure. Treatment should either be continued for at least 30 days or be used daily for 10 days, stopped for 10 days, then recommenced for 10 more days. Ivermectin has been shown to be effective as well (see discussion under cheyletiellosis). In most cases, if ivermectin has been used for four treatments at 10-14 day intervals, cases will be cured permanently unless they are reinfested from another animal. Ivermectin has also been used topically by applying directly into the ear canals. This method will not kill mites outside of the ear canal and therefore I prefer the systemic route (orally or by injection).

DEMODICOSIS

Demodex cati (*D. folliculorum var cati*) is a cigar-shaped mite which is believed to be a normal inhabitant of feline skin. The mite lives in hair follicles and occasionally in the sebaceous glands of the skin. The mite is only found on the surface of the skin when it travels between hair follicles. The life cycle begins with a spindle-shaped egg which develops into the first stage larvae, followed by nymphs, and finally the adult mite. The larvae have three pairs of legs, while the nymphs and adults have four pairs of legs. The mite is generally thought to feed on debris found within the hair follicle and perhaps material from the sebaceous glands. *Demodex cati* is considered a normal inhabitant of the skin in cats. *Demodex* mites are not contagious from one cat to another. Experimental attempts to transmit the mite and cause disease have been unsuccessful.

A second species of *Demodex* mite has also been observed but at this time remains unnamed. This mite is shorter than the long slender *Demodex cati* mite. Its life cycle has not been well studied.

A correct diagnosis is made by deep skin scrapings of the affected skin. It is often necessary to clip some of the hair so that an adequate sample can be obtained. The presence of a single mite will occasionally be seen but is considered a normal finding if just one is seen. In true cases of demodicosis, there will be several mites seen, and many times all four stages are found. Occasionally skin biopsies are required to find the mites.

There are several theories as to why mites which are considered normal inhabitants of the skin cause problems in individual cats. Underlying diseases which cause suppression of the immune system should always be considered in a cat with generalized demodicosis. A baseline health evaluation should include a fecal analysis, blood count, chemistry panel and thyroid hormone analysis as well as viral screens for feline leukemia, feline immu-

nodeficiency virus, and feline infectious peritonitis. Additional tests based on the results of the physical exam and initial screening may be needed to determine the underlying disease process.

There are two clinical types of demodicosis generally recognized, although in practice this difference is not always clear and may be more pertinent to dogs. Localized demodicosis appears as one to several single or isolated areas of patchy hair loss and is often accompanied by redness, scaling, (dandruff) or increased dark pigmentation. The increased pigmentation is a result of the inflammation as well as plugged follicles (blackheads) which give the skin a dark appearance. Blackheads are formed by obstruction of the hair follicle pore, which in this case is due to *Demodex* mites. The other form, which is known as generalized demodicosis, is much more extensive and severe. This classification is reserved for those cases which initially involve large areas of the body, or those cases in which the number of single lesions has increased. This classification is important because treatment and prognosis are different.

Treatment of localized demodicosis in a cat does not necessarily require aggressive or potentially dangerous therapy. Safe topical therapy includes benzoyl peroxide shampoos and/or gels. The shampoo should be allowed to have contact with the skin for a ten-minute period. Benzoyl

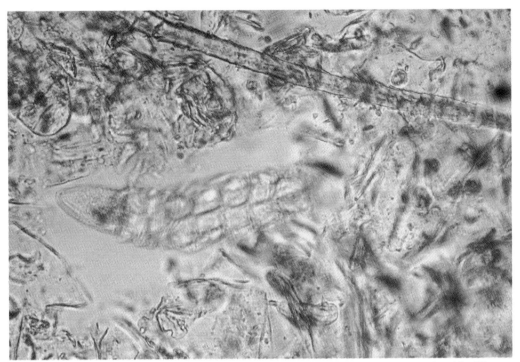

Microscopic view of the unnamed *Demodex* species. In appearance, this mite is noticeably different from *D. cati.*

peroxide has a follicular flushing action which helps remove the mite from the follicle, where it will quickly die. Underlying infections with feline leukemia virus, feline immunodeficiency virus, diabetes or other internal disease have been responsible for either treatment failures or worsening of the disease.

All crust should be removed, and the animal should be bathed with a shampoo containing benzoyl peroxide prior to dipping with lime sulfur. The cat should be dry at the time of dipping, to prevent dilution of the dip. The owner has the option of either toweling the cat dry, or applying the dip the following day. The dip should be sponged on the entire body. It's very important the animal not get wet between dips.

A 2% lime sulfur dip is the treatment (dip) of choice, and is applied at weekly intervals. Complete saturation of the skin and coat is needed for the most effective results. The cat is not toweled off but is allowed to drip dry. An Elizabethan collar will help prevent licking of the fur and ingestion of the dip. The use of rotenone, phosmet and malathion have all been used, but these drugs are potentially very dangerous to cats and should be used only as a last resort, if at all. A 0.025% solution of amitraz is the concentration recommended for treatment of demodicosis in *dogs*. However, this concentration in cats has been reported to cause serious side effects. Even a dose of 0.0125% solution can cause anorexia and the passage of a semifluid, malodorous feces for 24 hours. Therefore, amitraz should not be used in cats.

An additional drug which has shown promise in the treatment of this condition in dogs is ivermectin. There are several different treatment protocols available, but they have the advantage of possible oral administration. Clipping of the hair is not required as with dipping, although they may be used in addition to dips. Because cats with generalized demodicosis already have a suppressed immune system, drugs such as cortisone should not be used even if the patient is itchy. When excessive scratching is present, it may indicate the presence of a secondary bacterial infection. Treatment with antibiotics and antihistamines could then be helpful.

SCABIES

Scabies mites belong to the family Sarcoptidae, and the full name of the scabies mite affecting cats is *Notoedres cati*. The life cycle is spent entirely on the host and is complete in 17-21 days. These mites tunnel in the epidermis, which is the top layer of the skin. Female mites lay eggs behind them as they dig and crawl through the tunnel. The two pair of back legs are short and do not extend past the edge of the body. These mites are highly contagious by direct contact and can potentially be spread through kennel or hospital cages or grooming tools if they are not cleaned, dried, and sprayed with insecticides.

The most obvious symptom from the disease is intense itching, and often areas where the top layers of skin have been scratched away are seen. Because the mites prefer skin with little hair, the ears, face, elbows, abdomen, and hocks are areas that are affected more commonly. Clinically there is hair loss, yellow to red papules (small bumps), and crust. Patients which have been infested for longer periods of time develop very thickened skin with thick adherent scale and crust accumulations. The name "scabies" was derived from the word "scab."

The severe itching observed with scabies has several causes. Mechanical irritation to the skin from the burrowing female plays a role. There is, also, evidence that an allergic reaction to the mite and some of its excretions occurs. This further intensifies the itching and may account for the intense irritation and self-trauma created. Human volunteers experimentally infested with human scabies mites required a much shorter incubation time prior to developing symptoms the second time they were infested.

The diagnosis is confirmed by finding even one mite or egg on skin scrapings. The elbows, face, and ears are good places to scrape, and the scrapings should be extensive, with the accumulation of surface debris placed on the slide for examination. Scabies mites in cats seem to be more numerous and easier to find than their canine counterparts.

There are various topical and systemic medications used to treat scabies, and some are better than others. When severe crust is present, shampoos designed to remove crust will be necessary in addition to the mite treatment. Weekly lime sulfur dips of the entire body surface is a popular treatment although this product has an objectionable odor. Treatment for six to eight weeks, or two weeks past clinical remission is necessary. Ivermectin has been shown to be very effective in killing these mites. Although it is not approved for this use, it is generally considered safe and is the preferred choice of many veterinary dermatologists.

DERMANYSSIASIS (MANGE CAUSED BY THE POULTRY MITE, AKA RED MITE)

Dermanyssiasis is caused by the mite *Dermanyssus gallinae*. The mite generally feeds on fowl but has been known to infest dogs, cats, and man. The mite is gray to white but turns red from blood after feeding. The mite lives in cracks and crevices in the floor and walls during the day, and feeds on the host at night. Clinical signs include an itchy bumpy, crusty dermatitis of the head, back and limbs. Most affected animals have exposure to chicken houses. Almost all good insecticides safe for dogs which kill fleas will also kill these mites. Treatment should in-clude the environment, which is the source of the infestation.

TROMBICULIDIASIS (CHIGGER INFESTATION)

Trombiculidiasis is infestation with chigger mites. There are over 700 different species of chiggers. *Eutrombicula alfreddugesi* is the North American chigger. The adults do not live on or infest animals but instead live and feed on decaying vegetable debris. The larval stage is the only stage that affects mammals, and cats acquire them as they wander through wooded areas. If the larvae attach to the skin, they produce an itchy rash (papules, pimples and crust). The larvae are small (0.2-0.4 mm in length), bright orange in color, and attach tightly to the skin. Because the larvae only attach to the host for a few days, they may be gone by the time of examination. Most affected patients have a history of exposure to wooded areas. Most cases are seen in the central region of the United States during the summer and fall season. Treatment involves one to two parasiticidal dips, sprays or powder with any good, safe insecticide which is approved for flea control on cats.

ADDITIONAL READING

Ackerman, L.: *Pet Skin and Haircoat Problems*. Veterinary Learning Systems, Trenton, NJ, 1993, 216pp.

Muller, G.H.; Kirk, R.W.; Scott, D.W.: *Small Animal Dermatology*, W.B. Saunders Company, Philadelphia, 1989, 1007pp.

Dr. Alice Jeromin received a Bachelor of Science degree in pharmacy from the University of Toledo and was a practicing hospital pharmacist for 10 years before earning her Doctor of Veterinary Medicine Degree from The Ohio State University in 1989. She completed a three-year residency in veterinary dermatology and currently is in private practice in Cleveland, Toledo and Pittsburgh. She is actively involved in research in conjunction with Procter & Gamble in the area of canine skin lipids and sebaceous adenitis.

Bacterial and Viral Skin Infections

By Alice Jeromin, DVM
Diplomate, American College of Veterinary Dermatology
Veterinary Allergy & Dermatology Inc.
8979 Brecksville Rd.
Brecksville, OH 44141

INTRODUCTION

Few people would argue that cats keep themselves very clean. In essence, they are excellent groomers. It is for this reason that skin infections are infrequently seen in the cat.

In addition to the cat's ability to groom itself, the skin has certain inherent properties that help ward off infection. Hair is an important physical barrier, as is the stratum corneum, the uppermost layer of cells of the epidermis. Sebum, a lipid secreted by the sebaceous glands, not only keeps the skin soft and supple, but along with sweat, is made up of proteins and electrolytes that prevent excessive bacterial growth. Also present is the normal bacteria or the "good" bacteria that live on the skin. These make up the normal bacterial "flora" which include various species of staphylococci, micrococci, streptococci, and *Acinetobacter*. By occupying sites on the skin as part of the normal flora, invading foreign bacteria are unable to take up residence or "colonize."

BACTERIAL SKIN INFECTIONS

In most cases, trauma to the skin is required before disease-producing bacteria can take up residence and create infection. However, with certain bacteria, such as *Staphylococcus aureus*, no predisposing trauma is required. The bacterium itself is able to colonize and create an infection even in normal, intact skin. Other factors such as underlying disease may predispose the cat to skin infections.

In cats with recurrent skin infections, laboratory tests should be performed to evaluate for underlying internal diseases that might predispose the skin to more readily allow infection.

ABSCESSES

Of the few infections that do occur commonly, cat-bite abscess is a collection of pus under the skin that forms as a result of a puncture wound either by a cat bite or claw. Cat claws and teeth naturally harbor bacteria. This is implanted into the skin usu-

Different Types of Staphylococci that can be Recovered from Normal Cats.

Coagulase-Negative
S. capitis
S. epidermitis
S. haemolyticus
S. hominis
S. simulans*
s. cohnii
S. saprophyticus
S. sciuris. warneri
S. xylosus

Coagulase- Positive
S. hyicus
S. aureus**
S. intermedius

*most frequent isolate of normal cat skin
**most commonly isolated in skin infections of the cat

ally during a cat fight, and non-neutered males are most commonly involved. The bacteria grow and multiply while the body responds by creating inflammation in an attempt to fight off the "foreign" bacteria. Pus is the result of the body's attempt to dispel the bacteria. After a few days, the pus builds up pressure within the tissue and comes to a "head." The cat may be feverish, have a reduced appetite, and lack energy during this time. Usually, once the abscess comes to a head and then opens, the cat tends to feel better. The drainage is usually a combination of blood and pus and has the consistency of cream of tomato soup. Often the owners will notice a lack of appetite and lethargy *before* ever seeing the abscess. The cat is taken to the veterinarian, who by examination will detect the abscess and prescribe treatment. Ab-

scesses can occur anywhere but are most often seen on the face, neck, legs, or tailhead. Sometimes the original puncture marks go undetected until the veterinarian surgically explores the area and discovers the wound. The bacteria recovered from these abscesses are usually *Pasteurella,* or other microbes that reside in the mouths of cats. Other bacteria, including those found in the soil, can also be involved when cat claws are the cause.

Treatment of an abscess includes applying warm compresses to bring the abscess to a head. Oral antibiotics along with surgical drainage performed by the veterinarian are necessary to keep the abscess from filling up again. The veterinarian may need to "debride" or trim away the dead tissue to allow healing to occur. If the puncture wound is noticed soon after it occurs, early antibiotic therapy may prevent the abscess from forming altogether. However, once the abscess has formed, it should be allowed to "head up" and be drained before commencing antibiotics.

Abscesses are most commonly seen in non-neutered males that are allowed to roam. These individuals are most likely to fight for territory and sustain bite and claw wounds. One study showed that 80-90% of male cats that were neutered stopped their fighting and roaming. It is also important to remember that Feline Immunodeficiency Virus (FIV) is thought to be transmitted via cat bites particularly among fighting males. When abscesses are chronic or recur, it is important to consider infection with the Feline Leukemia Virus (FeLV), rare infections (Mycobacteria, Mycoplasma), puncture wound and foreign body reactions, and even cancer. Some deep abscesses can affect other

Abscesses are common in the cat and usually follow injury from cat fights.

tissues, including the lungs, bones, sinuses, and joints. Infections in these areas can be difficult to treat and require special radiography techniques, surgery, and the use of intravenous antibiotics.

Folliculitis

Bacterial infection of the hair follicles (folliculitis), although very common in the dog, is extremely uncommon in the cat. In fact, a recent study of 200 cats with skin problems found that only 5 of the 200 had hair follicle infections. The species of bacteria most commonly implicated is known as *Staphylococcus aureus*, or *Staph aureus* for short.

The appearance of cats with folliculitis is quite variable. Even though the folliculitis can look different in each cat, the majority of cats affected are older. The most common manifestation of bacterial folliculitis in the cat is feline acne. It occurs on the chin and appears as blackheads with swelling and pus accumulation. In one study of ten cats, numerous sites on the cat were swabbed and checked for bacterial growth. The chin area showed the highest amount of bacterial growth of all the sites sampled. Chin acne may occur because this is an area of the body that the cat is unable to keep clean. It is seen at any age and may be a chronic problem once it starts. Feline acne may respond to oral antibiotics and topical antiseptics. Drugs derived from vitamin A, including the topical compound Retin-A, have also been used.

Other cats with bacterial folliculitis may have crusty ears, surface peeling of the feet, and open sores with small crusts (miliary dermatitis). Usually, affected cats respond to 4-6 weeks of oral antibiotics and antibacterial shampoos. The best way to diagnose a bacterial folliculitis is to perform a skin biopsy (removal of a small piece of affected skin), although smears and cultures might also be useful. The skin removed in the biopsy procedure is preserved in formaldehyde and sent to a pathologist for evaluation. The pathologist then has the opportunity to evaluate all layers of the skin, from the deepest to the most superficial.

ATYPICAL BACTERIAL INFECTION
Nocardia

Another type of deep bacterial infection occurring in the skin can be due to environmental microbes such as *Nocardia* or mycobacteria. These organisms live in the soil and are introduced into the body by a puncture wound. Sometimes these organisms can grow very slowly and not show up for months or even years after initial contamination. This is analogous to human war veterans with shrapnel wounds that are dormant for many years and then cause problems later. In cats, the legs and chest are the most frequent areas affected. Wounds can appear as abscesses or open draining "holes" that tend not to heal. Diagnosis includes a culture of the drainage using special growth media. A biopsy

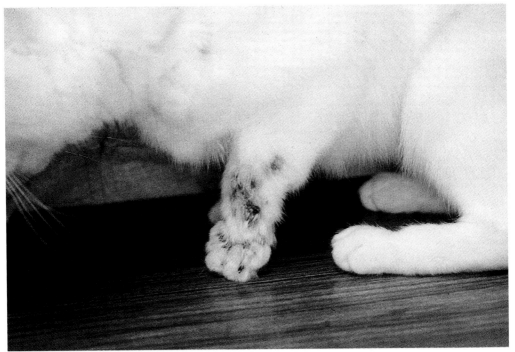

Nocardia infection is rare in the cat, but it is an important infection because it can be spread to people.

will also help determine if one of these rare infectious organisms is present. Therapy requires antibiotics given for long periods of time and sometimes surgery is necessary to prevent infection of other parts of the body, including bones. For example, an animal with *Nocardia* infection of the skin of the leg may require amputation if response to antibiotics given for long periods of time does not occur. Some cats with *Nocardia* infections have a weakened ability to fight off infection due to underlying disease. The patient should be checked thoroughly for any diseases that can impair the immune system and compromise the body's ability to fight infection.

Plague

Other less common bacterial infections affecting the cat include plague and leprosy. Plague is found in the warmer southwestern United States and is carried by fleas that live on affected rodents and squirrels. The infected fleas carry the disease to cats and dogs. Cats can also contract the disease by killing infected rodents. Bubonic plague causes abscesses in cats and can be transmitted to humans both by the fleas that carry it or by the infected pus from the abscess. Gloves should be worn when handling cats with abscesses in that particular geographic region, along with other safety precautions to prevent spread of the disease to humans. The signs of lethargy, lack of appetite, and abscesses occur the same as in cat-bite bacterial abscesses but plague can be lethal to some cats. Treatment includes antibiotics, drainage of abscesses, and flea control to reduce the transmission of the disease.

Leprosy

Leprosy in the cat is extremely rare in the United States and has mainly been reported in Canada, Australia, and New Zealand. Most affected cats are young. The disease can appear as an abscess or large "bump" that may or may not drain. Most are seen on the head, neck, or legs. A biopsy by the veterinarian is required for diagnosis.

VIRAL SKIN INFECTIONS

Although diseases caused by viruses such as Feline Leukemia Virus (FeLV) and Feline Immunodeficiency Virus (FIV) are of great concern in cats because they are deadly, few skin problems are seen in affected cats. As mentioned be-

fore, recurrent skin infections or abscesses can be seen with either viral infection. These infections tend to recur because the cat's immune system is not strong enough to fight off the infection which a normal cat is able to do. Cats with FIV infection also tend to get frequent bacterial and fungal infections in other areas like the mouth, gums, and feet.

A pox virus can also affect cats and is more common in England and Australia. Cats will have sores on their legs and head and may or may not be itchy. The sores usually heal without any treatment in 1-2 months. There have been reports of humans catching the virus when handling affected cats. The cat pox virus is extremely rare in the United States and Canada.

"Paw and mouth" disease in the cat is caused by a herpesvirus. The virus, along with causing respiratory symptoms, can cause ulcers in the mouth and on the foot pads. The cat may

> **Underlying Problems that can Predispose Cats to Infections.**
> 1. Trauma to the skin including abrasions, punctures, excessive wetting of the skin (maceration), insect bites, flea bites, excoriations from excessive itching
> 2. Foreign particles lodged in or under the skin such as foxtails, thorns, or glass.
> 3. Drugs such as corticosteroids, hormones and anti-cancer therapies can suppress the immune system and impair the body's own ability to fight infection.
> 4. Underlying internal medical problems such as feline leukemia, feline immunodeficiency virus infection (feline AIDS), feline infectious peritonitis, upper respiratory viral infection, diabetes mellitus, liver disease, kidney disease, cancer, malnutrition, internal parasites, Cushing's disease, or immune-mediated diseases such as pemphigus and systemic lupus erythematosus.

have a reduced appetite because of the mouth sores or even difficulty in walking if the sores affect the foot pads. Soft food should be offered, and antibiotics are usually prescribed by the veterinarian. Although antibiotics do not affect the virus, they help reduce the risk of secondary bacterial infections.

Lastly, there is always a question about whether or not humans can catch infectious diseases from their cats. Certainly humans with weakened immune systems (such as those receiving cancer chemotherapy or those with HIV) should take precautions when around any animal—either domestic pet or otherwise. Recently the organism that causes cat scratch disease (formerly cat scratch fever) was identified as *Rochalinaea henselae*, a rickettsial organism (rickettsiae are neither bacteria nor viruses, but are small organisms that can live within blood cells). This organism, *R. henselae*, can also cause a serious disease, bacillary angiomatosis, in humans with HIV. Cats can be asymptomatic and carry the organism. Fleas can also transmit the disease to people if they first feed on infected cat blood before they bite the person. Until more is learned about this organism and its method of transmission, susceptible humans need to take precautions with potentially infected cats and also use flea control on the cats routinely. Other infectious diseases that cats can transfer to humans include: toxoplasmosis, plague, *Pasteurella, Staphylococcus aureus*, streptococci, actinomycosis, catpox, dermatophilosis, tuberculosis, sporotrichosis, dermatophytes, and deep fungal infections.

SUMMARY

Cats are fastidious in their habits, but that doesn't make them immune to a variety of bacterial and viral infections. Cats that are allowed outdoors and which make contact with other cats are the most likely to develop serious infections. Some of these infections are transmissible to people and can cause serious problems, especially in individuals with AIDS. Proper vaccination, routine health care and an indoor lifestyle are the best ways to limit infections in cats.

ADDITIONAL READING

Muller, G.H., Kirk, R.W.; Scott, D.W.: *Small Animal Dermatology*, 4th Ed., W.B. Saunders, Philadelphia, 1989.

Sherding, R.G. (Ed.). *The Cat. Disease and Clinical Management.* Churchill Livingstone, New York, 1989.

White, S.: Pyoderma in five cats. *Journal of the American Animal Hospital Association*, 1991; 27(2).

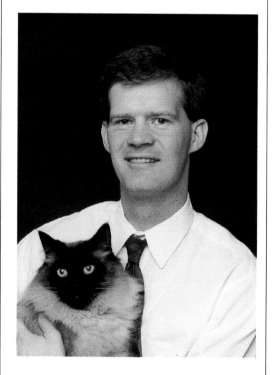

Dr. Jon D. Plant received his Doctor of Veterinary Medicine degree from Oregon State University in 1988. After a year in private practice, he completed a two-year residency in dermatology at the Animal Dermatology Clinic in Orange County, California. He is certified by the American College of Veterinary Dermatology. Dr. Plant and his associate see patients at the Animal Dermatology Specialty Clinic in three Los Angeles and Ventura County locations. He has lectured at numerous veterinary association meetings on veterinary dermatology subjects.

Ringworm and Other Fungal Infections

By Jon D. Plant, DVM
Diplomate, American College of Veterinary Dermatology
Animal Dermatology Specialty Clinic
1304 Wilshire Blvd.
Santa Monica, California 90403

INTRODUCTION

"Ringworm" is the common name given to fungal infections of the hair, skin, and nails caused by a group of organisms called dermatophytes. The medical name for these fungal infections is dermatophytosis. Three groups of fungi that include many species are possible causes of ringworm, but in the cat *Microsporum canis* is most often to blame. Most animal species, as well as humans, are susceptible to one or more types of ringworm organisms. Although each dermatophyte species is often found infecting a certain species of animal, this association is not rigid, allowing them to infect other species of animals as well when the opportunity arises. For instance,

Hair loss in a cat caused by the dermatophyte *Microsporum canis*.

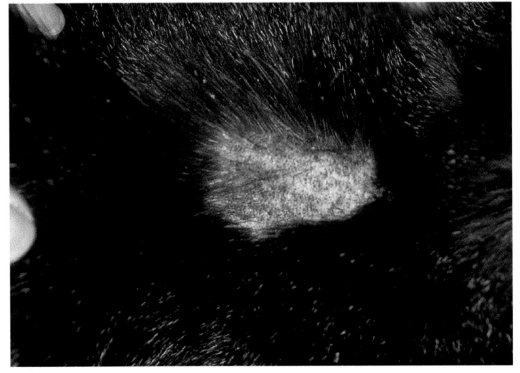

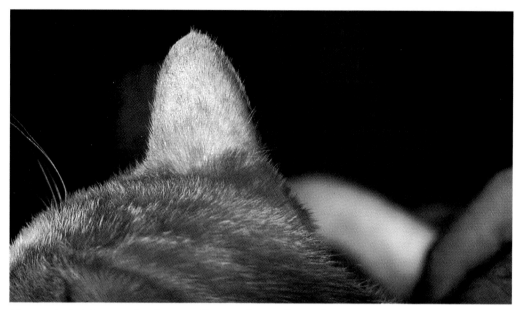

Fine scale, hair loss, and redness on the ear of a cat due to ringworm.

Microsporum canis primarily infects dogs and cats, but will also infect humans.

THE CLINICAL PICTURE

Dermatophytosis may take on several different appearances in cats. The most common form is an expanding, red, scaly, circular area in which the hair is lost. The center of these areas often becomes darker due to pigment production caused by the earlier inflammation. Although this type of pattern is suggestive of dermatophytosis, it is not the only disease that can take on this appearance, so an accurate diagnosis is important. Some cats will have only a solitary lesion, while others will develop a more widespread infection with multiple circular lesions blending together. In some cases, virtually the entire body is involved.

When a ringworm-infected area becomes swollen and is associated with pus, it is referred to as a kerion. Kerions are more inflamed than the more common, flat ringworm lesion. A rare form of ringworm occurs when dermatophytes are embedded within living tissue, deeper in the skin than the typical infection. In these so-called pseudomycetomas, the appearance is that of a lump under the skin. This type is more common in Persian cats than in other breeds.

When cats' nails are infected with dermatophytes (onychomycosis), the most common problem is crumbly, soft, deformed nails. The entire nail is sometimes shed. This type of infection can be very chronic and difficult to cure, but is luckily rare.

Another appearance that ringworm can take is that of widespread pimples and small bumps associated with erect-standing hairs and hair loss (a form of folliculitis—infection of the hair follicles). Because ringworm affects hairs as well as outer layers of the skin, hairs tend to be fragile and break off or pull out easily.

Obviously, ringworm can take on numerous appearances. Other syndromes which are sometimes caused by ringworm in cats include the so-called "miliary dermatitis" and chin acne. The areas of the body that are most commonly affected by "classic" ringworm in cats are the muzzle, head, pinnae (ear flaps), and extremities, including the tail.

Not all animals who come in contact with the fungi causing ringworm will develop the disease. What are the factors which make an animal more susceptible to ringworm infections? Any conditions that suppress an animal's ability to mount an effective immune response against dermatophytes makes those cats most susceptible to ringworm infection. These include: having an immature or aged immune system (very young or old animals); taking medications which suppress the immune system (like chemotherapy or chronic corticosteroids); and having a severe systemic illness (like feline leukemia virus infection). Other factors which may favor the development of ringworm in-

The hair loss and redness that is evident on this cat's toe was caused by *Microsporum canis*. This cat was also infected with feline immunodeficiency virus.

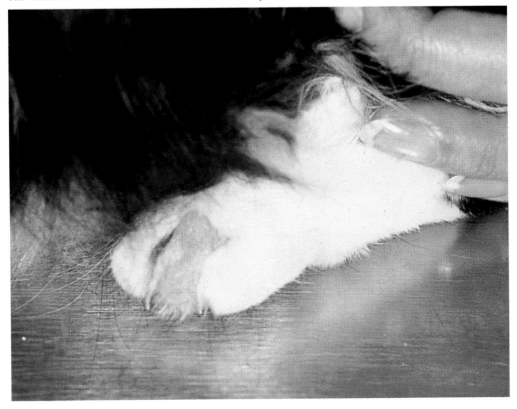

clude abrasions to the skin, high humidity, and exposure to especially infectious strains of dermatophytes.

Ringworm is a zoonotic disease, which means people can catch it from animals. However, just because one is in contact with a pet that has ringworm does not mean they will necessarily catch it. Some of the same factors which govern whether or not a pet is susceptible apply to humans as well. People on immunosuppressive medications, children, and elderly people are more susceptible. The risk can be minimized by washing one's hands after each handling of an infected cat and cleaning up the cat's surroundings well. A per- son who is known to be at increased risk of contracting ringworm should consider avoiding all contact with the cat until it is judged by their veterinarian to no longer be contagious. If one suspects they have ringworm, they should see their physician.

DIAGNOSIS

The diagnosis of ringworm is made by the veterinarian based upon clinical appearance and laboratory tests. A quick screening test involves illuminating the skin and hair with a Wood's light (a specific wavelength of ultraviolet light). Infections with some species of dermatophytes (principally *Microsporum canis* in cats) will sometimes cause the hair to

The ringworm affecting the chin and muzzle of this cat has some features of feline acne.

fluoresce under a Wood's light. However, the test is not very accurate because only about one-half of ringworm cases produce the characteristic apple-green fluorescence. Also, everything that glows is not necessarily ringworm. For instance, previous treatment of the lesion with one medication may cause a non-ringworm lesion to fluoresce while treatment with another may obliterate the fluorescence of a previously fluorescent ringworm lesion. Due to these inaccuracies, a Wood's light should only be used as a screening test, and a fungal culture or direct microscopic examination of the skin and hair should be taken from suspicious areas.

A fungal culture is performed by placing samples of hair, scale, or nails on a culture material designed to support the growth of dermatophytes, allowing for identification. The most common material, dermatophyte test media (DTM), also contains a color indicator which aids in the early detection of dermatophyte growth. Positive cultures are best confirmed by the veterinarian examining the growth microscopically for characteristic structures. In this way, the species of ringworm can be identified. It may take ten to fourteen days for the DTM to become positive, although in most cases it does so within seven days.

The veterinarian's direct microscopic examination of the hair or skin scraping can be aided by adding chemicals that dissolve

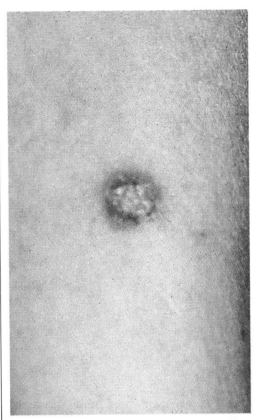

A circular lesion on the arm of a person who contracted ringworm from an infected pet.

the keratin, leaving any dermatophytes present easier to see. This test can provide conclusive results of ringworm more quickly than a fungal culture, but is more difficult to interpret.

TREATMENT

Treatment of infected cats after a diagnosis of ringworm has been made by a veterinarian may involve topical as well as oral therapy. Recent studies have suggested that many topical treatments used alone may not speed the resolution of ringworm infections in cats. Only oral antifungal therapy helped significantly in this set of studies.

Nonetheless, using antifungal shampoos, dips, and creams may help decrease the spread of ringworm to other pets, humans and the pet's environment. Most veterinarians recommend clipping the hair in and around affected areas so that those hairs containing dermatophyte spores are removed and discarded. While whole body clipping was once recommended, recent studies suggest that this is not helpful, and may actually spread the disease to uninvolved areas.

Topical creams often used on individual ringworm lesions include those containing miconazole, ketoconazole, and clotrimazole. Some studies have compared the effectiveness of topical therapy ingredients against various species of dermatophytes; however the results have differed depending on the study, and there is no clear cut winner. Creams are usually prescribed for use every 12 to 24 hours.

Antifungal shampoo ingredients that are commonly used to treat cats with ringworm include chlorhexidene and miconazole. Active ingredients of antifungal dips include enilconazole, lime sulfur, and chlorhexidene. Shampoos and dips are generally used every three to seven days.

Cats with extensive ringworm are often treated with oral antifungal medications. Griseofulvin is the standard treatment for cats. Side effects are uncommon,

but sometimes serious. Several human antifungal drugs (e.g., ketoconazole, itraconazole) have also been used successfully in cats. The veterinarian may choose an oral medication based on the severity of the case, any underlying diseases present, and other factors.

Cats with ringworm should receive treatment until their lesions are resolved and, ideally, a negative culture is obtained. This takes from three to ten weeks in average cases (and many months in nail infections). When an underlying condition is identified that is suppressing the immune system, it must be corrected, or the ringworm is likely to be chronic, recurrent, and hard to cure.

A vaccine has recently been marketed for the prevention and treatment of ringworm in cats. Its effectiveness is questionable, and as of the time of this writing, not widely recommended by veterinary dermatologists. The main criticism is that even though cats may look better after treatment with the vaccine, they are potentially still infected with dermatophytes. This means they are still capable of spreading the infection even though they look better. Further studies may still prove the vaccine to be of value, but, for now, it doesn't seem to be the answer we were looking for.

Cleaning and disinfecting the environment is an important part of effectively dealing with ringworm. All hard surfaces (floors and cages) should be cleaned with bleach, if possible. Bedding should be replaced or washed in hot water. Grooming supplies should be replaced or disinfected with bleach. Carpets should be thoroughly vacuumed daily. While steam cleaning may aid in removing infected hairs, it probably does not produce temperatures high enough to kill dermatophyte spores left in the carpet. Environmental contamination and the subsequent repeat infection of a cat can be a serious obstacle in a household or cattery where multiple animals are infected.

SPOROTRICHOSIS

Sporotrichosis is an uncommon fungal infection which can affect cats, other animals, and humans. The organism, *Sporothrix schenckii*, is normally found in decaying vegetation, and can be transferred to cats by thorn pricks, slivers, or bite wounds. Unlike the dermatophytes that cause ringworm, it can invade living tissue. This can lead to deep, draining wounds, swollen lymph nodes, and internal organ involvement. If a cat has sporotrichosis, it is a serious human health hazard, as numerous organisms can be found in the discharge which comes from their wounds. The veterinarian diagnoses this condition based upon examining the discharge, fungal cultures, or skin biopsy. Oral antifungal medication is necessary to treat sporotrichosis. If internal organs become infected, the disease is often fatal.

SUMMARY

Ringworm is a fungal infection of cats which may take on a number of different appearances. People can also catch it from their pets. The veterinarian uses a variety of tests to confirm the diagnosis, including culture, direct microscopic examination, and Wood's lamp evaluation. Treatment usually involves topical therapy, environmental cleanup, and sometimes, oral medication. A ringworm vaccine has become available recently but, for now, appears to be of limited value.

ADDITIONAL READING

Ackerman, L.: *Pet Skin and Haircoat Problems.* Veterinary Learning Systems, Trenton, New Jersey, 1993, 216pp.

Muller G.H., Kirk RW, Scott DW. *Small Animal Dermatology,* 4th Ed., 299-315, WB Saunders, Philadelphia, 1989.

This cat's face is infected with *microsporum canis*, which is visible under the fluorescence of a Wood's light.

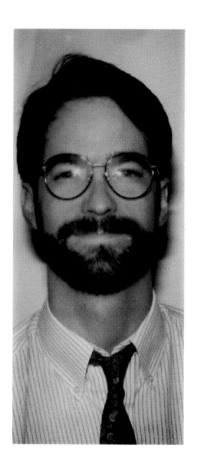

Dr. Dunbar Gram is a board-certified veterinary dermatologist. He received his undergraduate degree from Wesleyan University in Middletown, Connecticut and his Doctor of Veterinary Medicine degree (with high honors) from the College of Veterinary Medicine at Auburn University. Following veterinary school, he completed a one-year internship in small animal medicine and surgery at the University of Illinois. Dr. Gram then completed a residency in veterinary dermatology at North Carolina State University's College of Veterinary Medicine. He also served as a staff member there, as a clinical instructor in dermatology. Dr. Gram is currently involved in the process of training a dermatology resident and practicing his specialty in Hampton Roads and Richmond, Virginia.

Manifestations of Allergy in the Cat

By Dunbar Gram, DVM
Diplomate, American College of Veterinary Dermatology
Animal Allergy and Dermatology
P.O. Box 6858
Virginia Beach, VA 23450

INTRODUCTION

The clinical signs associated with allergies in cats are varied. They may range from a severe itch to a moderate itch or the appearance of excessive grooming. A crusty dermatitis and/or hair loss may also be present. The term "miliary dermatitis" is often used to describe this symptom. The gritty texture of debris on the surface of the skin is usually easier to feel than to see. It is important to note that miliary dermatitis is actually a symptom and not a disease. Many different skin diseases can cause the symptoms of miliary dermatitis so it cannot be considered an actual diagnosis. In some cats, non itchy sores or scabs may develop on the lip, back of the legs or skin of the stomach. The terms eosinophilic granuloma, eosinophilic ulcer (rodent ulcer) and eosinophilic plaque are often used to describe these symptoms. As with miliary dermatitis, these terms should be considered as symptoms of a disorder, not a diagnosis. An underlying cause still must be determined. Diseases other than allergies may also be present. In addition to dermatologic problems, changes in behavior, including irritability, aggressiveness, nervousness and other symptoms, may occur. Like dogs, cats may be allergic to fleas, food substances or inhaled allergens such as dust and pollens.

The most common types of allergies seen in cats include flea allergy, inhalant allergy (similar to hay fever in humans) and food allergy. Contact allergy is quite rare. The hallmark clinical sign of allergies is itching. Often these different types of allergies may have symptoms that look alike with only subtle differences in history, distribution of clinical signs or response to therapy. Flea and mite infestations as well as fungal infection may also mimic the clinical signs of allergies. The basic physiologic aspect of the different types of allergies is similar. The allergy-causing substance gains entrance into the body either through the skin, lungs or digestive tract. In normal animals, these substances (called allergens) do not cause the individual any problems. In affected animals, the allergens cause an exaggerated immune response resulting in various clinical signs. These clinical signs will be discussed individually with each allergy.

In many cases, fleas complicate the task of identifying other causes of itching such as allergies. Often, a pet's itching may be due to a combination of fleas and other factors. The clinical signs of allergic inhalant dermatitis and food allergy can be very similar to symptoms associated with flea-associated dermatitis. Without adequate flea control, it can be difficult to determine how much a pet would itch if only the factors unrelated to fleas were present. Many people are under the false impression that if fleas or flea bites do not affect humans, fleas are not a problem for their pet. Most fleas prefer dogs and cats in-

stead of humans. Mild to moderate flea infestations may not actually result in a problem for the humans in the house, but a relatively few number of fleas can cause a significant problem for the animals in the house. If adequate flea control is not effective in controlling itching, other possible causes should be considered.

FLEA ALLERGY

In contrast to the non-flea-allergic cat that itches only when exposed to several fleas, a flea-allergic cat can suffer from extreme discomfort associated with a single flea. The flea-allergy reaction occurs when a flea bites a flea allergic cat and exposes the cat's immune system to flea saliva. The ensuing allergic reaction can occur very quickly, and

An example of self-trauma due to excessive licking, which is associated with allergies. Notice the hair loss over the "rump."

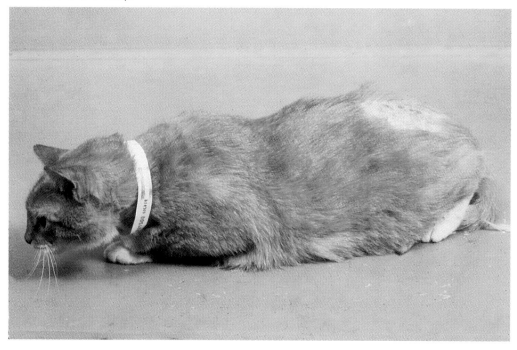

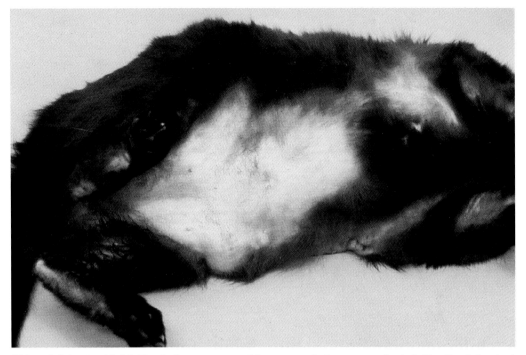

This cat did not exhibit licking in the presence of its owners, but was secretively licking its abdominal area. These cats are sometimes referred to as "closet" lickers.

may last for many days. Clinical signs are often more severe near the area of the flea bite, but can also occur in distant locations. Itching, redness, small bumps (miliary dermatitis), eosinophilic granuloma complex, and self-induced trauma result. As with flea infestation, the most severely affected area is often on or near the rump and neck regions. Excessive licking or chewing of other parts of the body can be seen with flea allergy as well as other allergies.

Eradication of fleas is the most important aspect of controlling a flea allergic cat. Please see the discussion of fleas and flea control elsewhere in this book for more information on flea control. Cats are more sensitive than dogs to certain flea products. It is important to only use products that specifically state they are safe for use on cats when implementing a flea control program. Consultation with a veterinarian concerning potential toxicities and effectiveness is strongly recommended when implementing any flea control program.

ALLERGIC INHALANT DERMATITIS

Allergic inhalant dermatitis is also called atopy. This disease involves allergic reactions to various pollens (grasses, trees, molds and weeds) as well as other substances with microscopic allergens that can be inhaled, such as dust and dust mites. These substances interact with the cat's immune system primarily through the lungs. Humans with inhalant allergies primarily suffer from symptoms such as runny noses, irritated eyes and sneezing. Cats usually manifest this type of allergy by exhibiting the symptoms described in the introduction to this chapter, such as scratching, rubbing, licking, biting or excessively grooming themselves. The rump, neck and skin of the abdominal region are commonly affected. Some cats develop a crusty dermatitis or so-called miliary dermatitis that may or may not itch. Red sores that weep or ooze (such as those associated with eosinophilic granuloma complex), affecting the lips and other parts of the body, have also been associated with allergies. The symptoms may start after the age of adolescence and initially cause problems during a particular season. With time, the clinical signs become more severe and may last all year long.

Although controlling exposure to the allergens that cause flea, food and contact allergy is often possible, it is very difficult to control exposure to substances in the air. If the clinical signs cause the pet to be uncomfortable, medical therapy may be necessary. If the symptoms do not adequately respond to medical therapy or side effects of the drugs occur, allergy testing should be considered. The three main forms of non-specific medical therapy are: corticosteroids, antihistamines, and nutritional supplements.

Corticosteroids are hormones that suppress inflammation in the body, including the inflammation and itch associated with

The same cat as pictured on the preceding page. Intradermal allergy testing revealed many positive reactions.

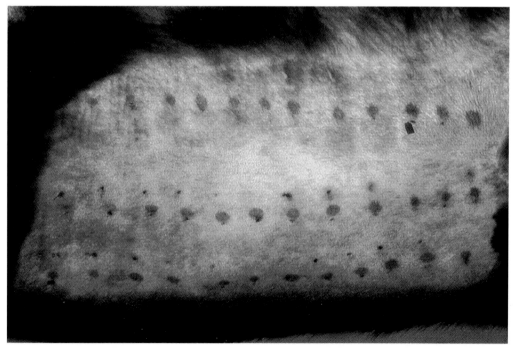

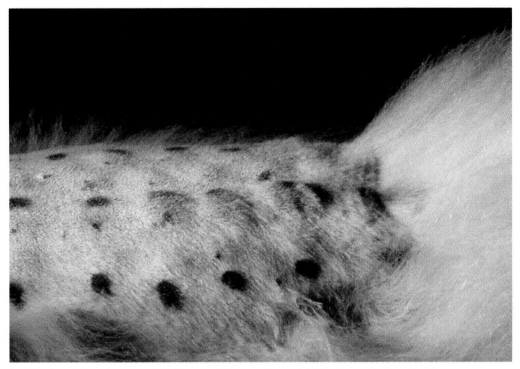

A side view of another cat exhibiting positive reactions with intradermal allergy testing.

allergies. Although corticosteroids are never drugs that should be used casually, it is true that cats are very tolerant to their effects. Cats handle these drugs very efficiently and do much better than dogs or people would with comparable doses. For this reason, they are commonly used in the treatment of feline allergies. Monitoring is still recommended on a regular basis because cats are not completely immune to adverse effects, including diabetes mellitus.

Antihistamines can be effective in cat inhalant allergies, as they are for treating people with hay fever. Just like people, cats can have variable responses to antihistamines; certain products are more effective for some cats than others. The most commonly used antihistamines are chlorpheniramine (Chlortrimeton™ and clemastine (Tavist™), although neither are licensed for this use in cats.

Nutritional supplements can also be helpful in relieving itchiness in allergic cats. Special fatty acid supplements that are available from veterinarians and some pet supply outlets have combinations of gamma-linolenic acid (from evening primrose or borage) and eicosapen-taenoic acid (from fish oil), which help relieve inflammation naturally. Although the ultimate success rate of this therapy has not been precisely determined, it is quite apparent that many cats do benefit anecdotally.

When non-specific therapy is insufficient or unacceptable, specific tests are needed to determine the true cause of the allergy and to formulate appropriate immunotherapy (allergy shots). Currently, two different methods for allergy testing exist. Skin testing for allergies involves the intradermal injection of small amounts of various types of diluted purified allergen extracts and monitoring for a wheal (a localized reaction that looks like a hive or welt). Skin testing, or intradermal skin testing as it is also known, is similar to the allergy test that most people are familiar with being used for allergy testing humans. Blood testing is a relatively new type of test which involves obtaining a sample of blood and submitting it to a laboratory that performs the specialized testing. After the positive reactions identified with the allergy test are correlated with the history, the immunotherapy solution (allergy extract) can be formulated. This solution contains a mixture of specific allergens. The exact mix of allergens is different for each patient and is based upon the pet's history, positive allergy test results, the veterinarian's (and/or the laboratory's) clinical experience in treating allergies and other considerations. Injections of immunotherapy solution of allergy extract are also referred to as allergy shots. This type of allergy shot should not be confused with steroid or cortisone injections, which are quite different.

The treatment of allergies is complicated, and the likelihood of success with immunotherapy (or allergy shots) can be affected by a number of factors. The allergy tests themselves can be technically complicated and are best interpreted by a veterinarian who has received specialized training in the treatment of allergic skin diseases. The most precise results are obtained with the use of individual allergens rather than groups of allergens. The disadvantage of using groups of mixed allergens becomes apparent while considering the results of the test. When a group of mixed allergens has a negative test, all allergens in the group or mix are considered to be negative. This is unfortunate because if the allergens were tested individually, one of the allergens could actually show a true positive test result. Conversely, a group of mixed allergens that test positive may actually contain an individual allergen that would truly test negative if individual testing were performed.

The less accurate nature of using groups or mixes for allergy testing complicates the formulation of the immunotherapy solution and may inadvertently lead to omission of an important allergen in the allergy extract. Additionally, the practice of using groups or mixes could lead to the inclusion of allergens which are not relevant, thereby diluting the concentration of the important allergens. Both situations are likely to reduce the efficacy of the treatment. Studies in dogs indicate that the highest success rate with immunotherapy is achieved through the use of the

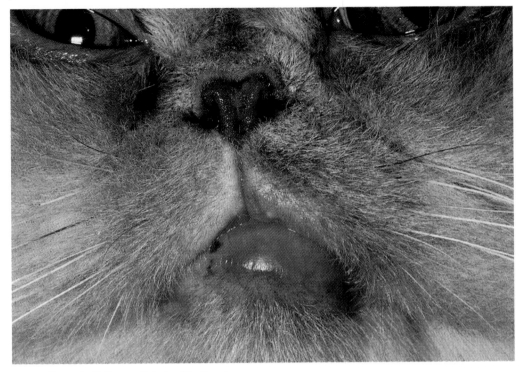

A cat with a "fat lip" associated with allergies.

most precise testing and the highest concentration of immunotherapy solution. Grouping of allergens should be avoided in either type of allergy test and the highest concentration of immunotherapy solution that can safely be used should be administered as an allergy shot.

Skin testing allows for relatively inexpensive identification of individual allergens. Many blood tests are also at a disadvantage because they test for groups or mixes of allergens. Although it is possible to utilize groups or mixes of allergens with skin testing, most allergens are tested for individually. The concentration of the immunotherapy (allergy extract) solution can also vary with the type of test performed and as previously discussed can affect the success rate. Skin testing has numerous advantages over blood testing, but is complicated to perform and interpret. Both types of test are best performed under the guidance of a veterinarian with training in allergic skin diseases. In summary, intradermal skin testing is the historical standard and the preferred method for allergy testing. Some veterinary dermatologists find the combined use of both tests to be useful.

FOOD ALLERGY

Food allergy is a relatively rare disease and generally overemphasized by many pet food companies as a cause of itching. Intense itching of the face and head is a common symptom, but the clinical signs can be virtually indistinguishable from those seen in allergic inhalant dermatitis. Itchy cats should be evaluated for mites because mite infestation may mimic food allergy. The symptoms are not usually associated with a change in diet, may start at any age and do not vary with the time of year or season.

Various tests are available for assistance in diagnosing food allergy. However, neither blood tests or the skin tests are very helpful in confirming the diagnosis. While positive reactions are often seen, they are usually not clinically important. Falsely positive reactions may lead to the incorrect belief that a pet is very food allergic. Negative reactions offer slightly more useful information and indicate that a pet can likely tolerate a specific food substance. Most veterinary dermatologists do not recommend blood tests or skin tests for the diagnosis of food allergy. The best way to diagnose a food allergy is with the proper use of a hypoallergenic diet. This diet should have undergone clinical trials which verify its hypoallergenic nature. Manufacturer claims that a diet contains certain substances does not indicate that the diet is truly hypoallergenic.

In order for an animal to be allergic to a food substance, the animal must have been exposed to the substance before. Lamb is a good example. There is absolutely nothing magic about lamb and food allergy. Simply, most cats have not eaten lamb before

This patient has developed a severe eosinophilic ulcer (also known as rodent ulcer) of the lip.

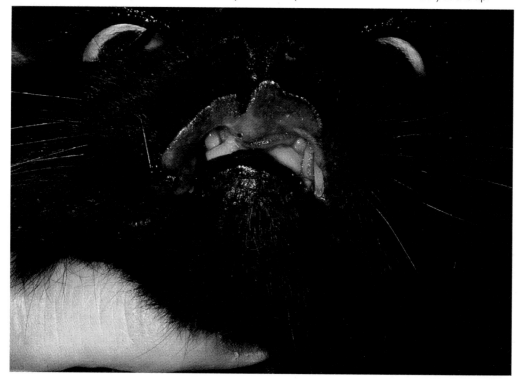

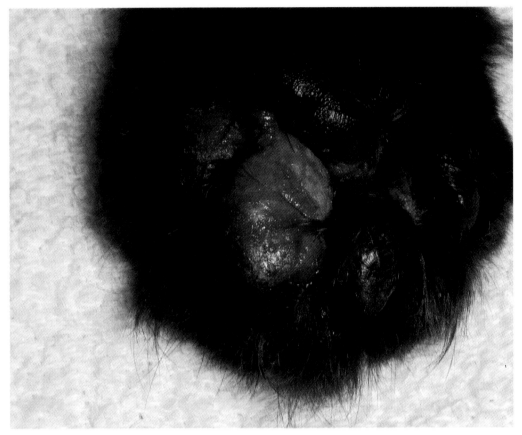

The same cat as pictured on the opposite page. In addition to the facial ulcer, it also exhibits an eosinophilic granuloma on one of its foot pads.

and therefore cannot be allergic to it. A cat that has eaten lamb as part of its normal diet may actually be allergic to lamb. For years, lamb has been recommended by veterinarians as an alternative to beef or chicken as a protein source in the diet of cats suspected of having food allergy. Unfortunately, the indiscriminate use of lamb in many cat foods has further complicated the necessary steps required to diagnose food allergy.

Before initiating a hypoallergenic diet, a pet owner must understand that it is a true diagnostic test and should not be undertaken without conviction. Many times a hypoallergenic dietary trial is not strictly followed, and the pet is allowed continued exposure to table scraps or beef flavored treats, rawhides and chew toys. Vitamin supplements that contain meat flavorings should be substituted with a comparable product that does not contain these potential allergens. Failure to observe these requirements invalidates the test and results in unnecessarily exposing the pet to another potentially allergenic substance, such as lamb. This unnecessary exposure may preclude the use of such substances from being utilized in the future when a more strictly followed hypoallergenic diet is considered.

In summary, a properly performed hypoallergenic dietary trial is the most appropriate test for diagnosing food allergy. An improperly performed hypoallergenic dietary trial may actually do more harm than good because it may complicate future attempts at diagnosing food allergy. Diets containing certain substances such as lamb are not necessarily hypoallergenic. Only diets which have undergone clinical trials confirming their hypoallergenic nature should be used during the testing period. Unfortunately, an extremely small number of diets have undergone these trials. The hypoallergenic diet should be continued until the cat improves or for a duration of 8-10 weeks. If a pet improves while eating a hypoallergenic diet, the original diet should be reintroduced and the pet monitored for the return of itching within 7-14 days. Sometimes the itching may return within a matter of hours. This reintroduction of the original diet is a critical part of the test and helps prove that the improvement was due to the food and not due to coincidence. Once a food allergy is confirmed in this manner, the patient should be placed back on the successful hypoallergenic diet until the itching is no longer present. The cat may be maintained on this diet (provided it is well balanced and complete) or placed on another

diet and monitored for recurrence of itching. It is at this time that the use of diets, which have not undergone true clinical trials proving their hypoallergenic nature, may be considered for the individual pet. Introduction of potential allergenic substances may also be added individually to the proven hypoallergenic diet. This protocol allows for more precise identification of the offending food substance.

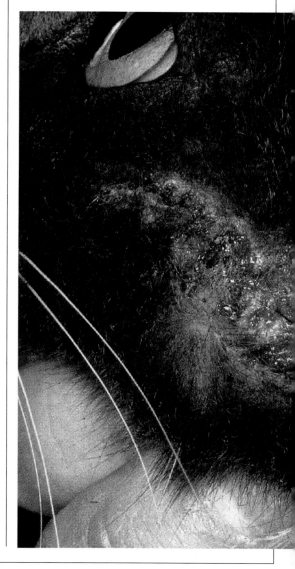

SUMMARY

The identification and treatment of allergies in cats can be both frustrating and challenging. It is important to ensure that other diseases which mimic allergies are not present. Nonspecific medical control of allergies can be helpful while investigating what type of allergy is present. Cats tend to tolerate steroids better than dogs, but side effects can occur. Hormonal drugs such as Ovaban® should be avoided because of their potential to cause diabetes and mammary tumors. The use of nonsteroidal medications (antihistamines and fatty acids) should be considered and discussed with a veterinarian or veterinary dermatologist.

ADDITIONAL READING

Ackerman, L.: *Pet Skin and Haircoat Problems.* Veterinary Learning Systems, Trenton, New Jersey, 1993, 216pp.

Bettenay, S.: Diagnosing and treating feline atopic dermatitis. *Veterinary Medicine,* 1991, May; 488-496.

Wills, J.M.: Diagnosing and managing food sensitivity in cats. *Veterinary Medicine,* 1992, September: 884-892.

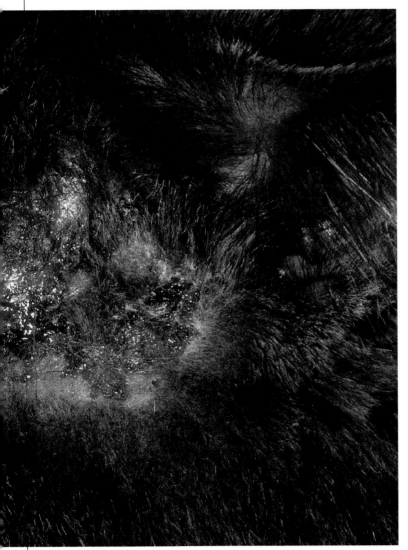

Another example of eosinophilic dermatitis. This cat is affected on the side of its face.

Dr. Bruce L. Hansen is a Diplomate of the American College of Veterinary Dermatology and is a practicing veterinary dermatologist in Springfield, Virginia. He received his Doctorate in Veterinary Medicine from the Veterinary School at the University of Missouri in 1980 and went on to do a dermatology residency program at the University of Pennsylvania. Dr. Hansen served one year as Clinical Instructor in Veterinary Dermatology at the University of Pennsylvania prior to opening Dermatology and Allergy Services for Animals. He is currently serving as an adjunct clinical professor for the Virginia-Maryland Regional Veterinary School.

Problems with Hair Loss

By Bruce L. Hansen, DVM
Diplomate, American College of Veterinary Dermatology
Dermatology and Allergy Services for Animals
6651-F Backlick Rd.
Springfield, Virginia 22150

INTRODUCTION

Hair loss that results in baldness is defined as alopecia. Alopecia may occur in small patches or be generalized and involve large areas of the body. Hair loss is a very common problem in pets and can be caused by a variety of diseases. Because animals are covered in a thick luxuriant hair coat, diseases that cause hair loss in the cat are very noticeable and distressing to the pet owner.

What causes hair to fall out? With modern medicine you might think that you should be able to call the local veterinarian to get a pill or shot to cure the alopecia. Unfortunately, hair loss is only a symptom shared by many different diseases. The patterns of hair loss in many diseases are identical, so that even the trained eye of a veterinarian cannot identify the cause of alopecia in the pet; numerous laboratory tests are often required. Some cases are so complex that a veterinary dermatologist is needed to correctly diagnose the cause of the alopecia and prescribe appropriate treatment.

CAUSES

Cats develop hair loss in many of the same ways as dogs, but grooming habits in cats make virtually all dermatologic changes look similar.

Therefore, identifying the source of hair loss is often much more difficult than in the dog.

Infections and Infestations

Diseases that affect the hair and hair follicle can cause patchy to widespread hair loss. Hair follicle infections loosen hair and eventually dislodge it to result in hair loss. In the cat, hair follicule infections are usually due to bacteria found in the cat's mouth. This is because bite wounds are a very common way that cats develop bacterial skin infections.

Demodicosis is a skin condition

Cat with ringworm (dermatophytosis) resulting in hair loss on top of the head.

caused by infestation with *Demodex* mites. However, demodectic mange in the cat appears to be significantly different than the same condition seen in dogs. In the cat, demodicosis can result in folliculitis like that seen in the dog, usually in cats whose immune system has been debilitated by disease. It can also appear as a severely itchy disease not associated with hair follicles (these cats are not immunosuppressed). Both types result in hair loss.

Although the other forms of folliculitis (demodicosis and bacterial folliculitis) are seen less often in the cat than the dog, fungal infections, particularly ringworm (dermatophytosis), are seen much more commonly in the cat. Ringworm is a frequent cause of patchy hair loss in the kitten, and some-

times seen in older cats. As animals get older, they generally become more resistant to fungal infection. Generalized ringworm in the older cat is a warning sign that something or some disease may be severely depressing the cat's immune system, and every older cat with a fungal infection should be examined closely for the presence of internal disease. Because ringworm is contagious to people, all cats with hair loss should be examined for the presence of dermatophytosis. Furthermore, ringworm survives for long periods of time in the environment or surroundings as spores that can affect generation after generation of animals and people. Because these spores are extremely difficult, if not impossible, to kill, every effort should be made to detect all cases of ringworm as early as possible to prevent

This cat has severe flea allergy dermatitis, which has resulted in the extensive loss of hair.

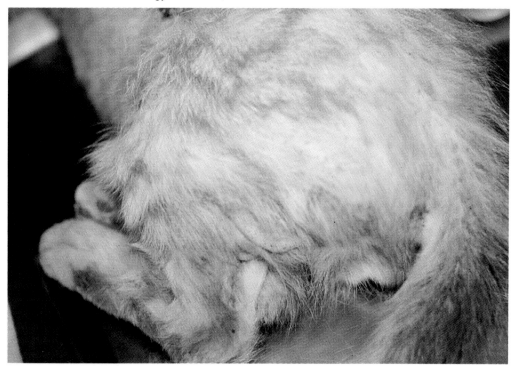

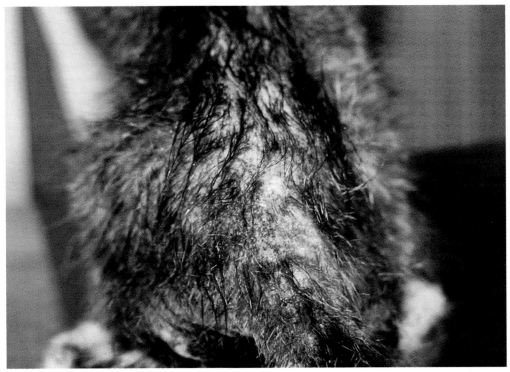

This cat shows evidence of severe chewing over the back. The cause is a cheyletiellosis infestation.

further contamination of the surrounding environment.

Other Causes

Diseases causing damage or death to the hair or hair follicle (which is the pore in which the hair grows), and diseases causing excessive traction or pulling on the hair can result in hair loss. Cats with hormonal problems, from either too much or too little of certain hormones, often have fur that stops growing and falls out. The resultant hair loss is termed an endocrine alopecia (endocrine implying a hormonal nature). Underlying causes of endocrine alopecias in the cat include Cushing's syndrome, hypothyroidism and and a variety of sex hormone imbalances. Endocrine alopecia is characterized by hair loss without evidence of any itching. While many cat owners feel their cat does not lick, scratch, or groom themselves excessively, in reality their cats are just very secretive about their excessive grooming habits. Therefore, extreme caution should be used before assuming a cat has an endocrine hair loss. To the naked eye, all forms of hormonal hair loss are identical. The only way to identify the correct hormonal abnormality is to perform specific blood tests and to construct a careful history of other clinical symptoms.

Conditions or events that are very stressful to pets can result in a sudden generalized hair loss called telogen or anagen dysfluxion. Examples would include loss of hair after a very high fever, or the sudden loss of hair in a mother cat (queen) after delivering and nursing a litter of kittens. Some medications or toxins (poisons) can cause hair death and subsequent hair loss. In people, hair loss of this type would include hair loss associated with chemotherapy. In animals, the rodent poison thallium causes rapid complete hair loss (and later death) if ingested in sufficient quantities.

Autoimmune skin diseases are diseases in which the body attacks its own skin. The result is destruction of skin and hair follicles with consequent hair loss and scaling. Autoimmune skin diseases do occur in cats on an infrequent basis with pemphigus foliaceus and cutaneous lupus erythematosus being the most common autoimmune dis-

eases encountered. Every effort should be made to ensure the correct diagnosis is made, as treatment for autoimmune skin disease would have disastrous effects on a cat with a skin infection (folliculitis). Finally, diseases like toxic epidermal necrolysis and erythema multiforme are conditions in which the immune system attacks the skin (which is an innocent bystander), sometimes destroying the entire epidermis (or top layer of skin), completely obliterating all hair follicles in its path. The result is not only areas of hair loss but also complete ulceration of the skin. The most common cause for toxic epidermal necrolysis and erythema multiforme is a drug allergy. From a clinical standpoint these diseases can closely resemble

An example of notoedric mange infestation.

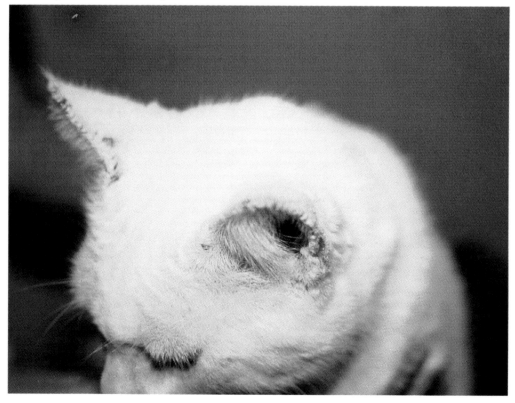

demodicosis, ringworm, and bacterial folliculitis. Because treatment of autoimmune skin disease requires decreasing the body's immune response (to decrease the body's ability to attack itself), extreme care needs to be taken to ensure the correct diagnosis is made. Otherwise, if a bacterial folliculitis, ringworm or demodicosis was present, the treatment for autoimmune skin disease would tremendously worsen the disease.

Skin diseases not associated with hair follicles can cause hair loss by causing inflammation that secondarily affects hair and hair follicles. Cutaneous lymphosarcoma and other skin cancers (such as squamous-cell carcinoma) can spread rapidly and cause severe inflammation, destroying and pushing hair follicles aside, leaving bald nodules or growths on the skin surface. Unfortunately, treatment for most of these skin cancers is usually unrewarding.

Excessive itching (pruritus) exhibited by scratching, chewing, licking and biting of the fur, is the most frequent process by which cats develop alopecia. As mentioned earlier, cats are often secretive about their grooming, and a large majority of cat owners are unaware that their itchy cats are scratching at all. Furthermore, itchy cats can produce hair loss by licking excessively, producing bald skin as smooth as a newborn baby's "bottom." Therefore, every effort should be made in non-itchy, partially bald cats to determine if the cat is truly non-itchy, or if they are a "closet" licker. In many cases this requires a collar

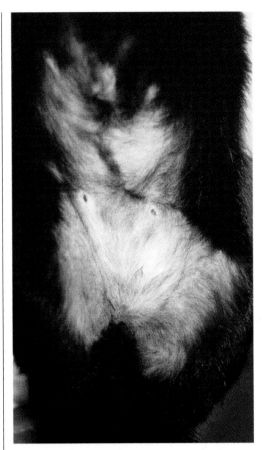

A cat with psychogenic alopecia on its belly.

(Elizabethan collar) to be placed around the cat's neck for 30 days. If the cat has been excessively grooming the bald areas, a short stubble of hair will be seen growing from the hairless area.

Fleas are a common reason for excessive scratching and grooming in cats. Again, cats often manifest itching by grooming excessively. Therefore, many times flea populations on the cat are kept to very low levels as the cat will physically remove most of the fleas by grooming, making a flea infestation look much less severe than it is. Furthermore, because cats lick themselves constantly while grooming, all flea products applied to the cat's skin are quickly licked off leaving no residual protection against fleas. Therefore, treatment of flea bite dermatitis/allergy in a household with cats should involve limiting the cat's environment (keeping it indoors exclusively), and focusing primarily on treatment of the house (although concurrent treatment of the pets is necessary to reduce their clinical symptoms). Additionally, because flea eggs are quite resistant to insecticides, and because complete flea eradication of an environment is impossible, multiple treatments may be needed on a regular basis.

Otodectes cynotis (ear mites) are a common cause of itching (and hair loss of the neck and ear region), and in rare cases they have been reported to be a cause of generalized itching and hair loss in the cat. *Cheyletiella* mites (cheyletiellosis), *Notoedres cati* mites (notoedric mange), lice (pediculosis), and chiggers (trombiculidiasis) are other parasites that sometimes cause itching-induced fur loss in the cat. Some of these parasites can transiently affect humans, so prompt veterinary care is recommended. Fortunately, treatment for these conditions is usually safe and very effective.

Exceptionally nervous cats, or cats emotionally disturbed by something in their environment, may begin to excessively groom themselves to release tension—resulting in psychogenic alopecia. However, hold the Prozac—all causes of itching in the cat can look exactly like psychogenic alopecia. Therefore, cats should always be proven to be obsessive, overly nervous, distraught, or psychotic before they are labeled as having a psychogenic alopecia.

Allergic dermatitis is common in the cat. Flea allergy is by far the predominant type of allergy encountered. Again, cats manifest allergy by excessive grooming. Therefore, finding evidence of a flea infestation in the strongly flea-allergic cat is next to impossible. Subsequently, cats with excessive grooming may be suffering from severe flea allergy without the owners even knowing that fleas are present. This reinforces the need for thorough dermatologic evaluation, potentially with a veterinary dermatologist, for these itchy felines.

Following flea allergy, food allergy is the next most common type of allergy that occurs in the cat, followed by allergic inhalant dermatitis. Food allergy is difficult to diagnose in that often the cat has been eating the offending diet for over two years before the allergy develops. Additionally, the offending allergen (the object to which the animal is allergic) is an ingredient of the diet rather than a brand of cat food. Because many cat foods share the same ingredients, simply switching from one brand of cat food to another is ineffective in identifying the presence of food allergy. Finally, to document a food allergy requires the feeding of a special hypoallergenic diet (a diet composed of proteins that are novel to most cats) for a period up to ten weeks. Therefore, extreme diligence and patience is required to make a diagnosis of a food allergy.

Allergic inhalant dermatitis in the

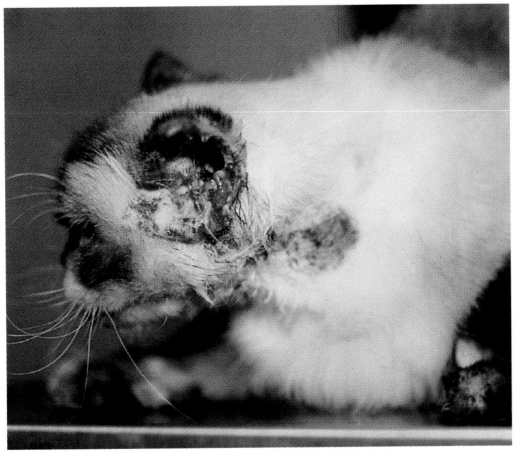

Severe itching and hair loss on the face of this Himalayan cat are due to a food allergy.

cat is caused by exposure to pollens, molds, and dust mites that are inhaled (and to a lesser extent absorbed from the skin surface). This type of allergy is the third most common allergy (behind flea and food allergies) seen in the cat. To diagnose inhalant allergies in the cat, skin tests are performed, similar to those used for people and dogs. A small patch of fur is shaved, and potential allergy-causing substances (allergens) are injected into the skin in small amounts. Positive reactions are usually evident within about 10-15 minutes.

Allergic contact dermatitis (an allergic reaction to materials contacting the cat's skin) does occur, but only rarely since the cat's long hair coat acts as protection against prolonged contact with potentially allergenic substances.

Eosinophilic granuloma complex is an incompletely understood group of dermatologic diseases capable of causing hair loss from excessive itching. This disease complex is characterized by ulcerated growths (particularly of the upper lip) to well demarcated, raised, extremely reddened, and irritated lesions or sores usually on the cat's abdomen and thighs. Veterinary dermatologists

Your cat's coat can be a good indicator of its overall health. Abyssinians photographed by Isabelle Francais.

feel many of the cases of eosino-philic granuloma complex are manifestations of an allergy, or to a reactive process from an insect bite (such as a mosquito).

SUMMARY

Numerous diseases are capable of causing excessive hair loss in the dog and cat. Many are identical in the pattern and appearance of the hair loss. Furthermore, animals can suffer from several diseases that cause hair loss at the same time (for example, animals with flea allergy can develop bacterial folliculitis;

hypothyroid dogs can catch sarcoptic mange, etc.), making evaluation extremely difficult. Therefore, a thorough medical examination is mandatory in all causes of hair loss in the dog and cat.

ADDITIONAL READING

Ackerman, L.J.: *Pet Skin and Haircoat Problems.* Veterinary Learning Systems, Trenton, New Jersey, 1993, 216pp.

Muller, G.H.; Kirk, R.W.; Scott, D.W.: *Small Animal Dermatology.* W.B. Saunders Co., Philadelphia, 1989, 1007pp.

Cat with nodular cobblestone-like growths and hair loss on the inside of the thigh due to eosinophilic granuloma complex.

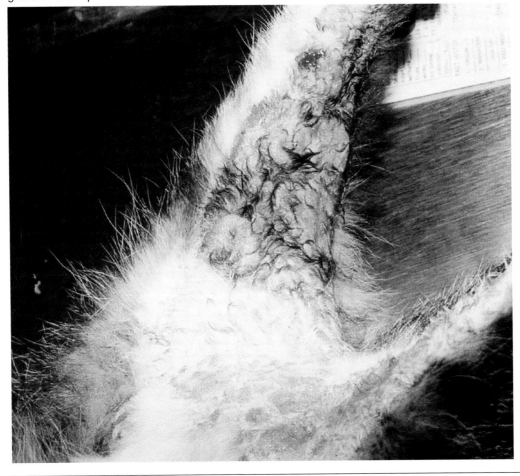

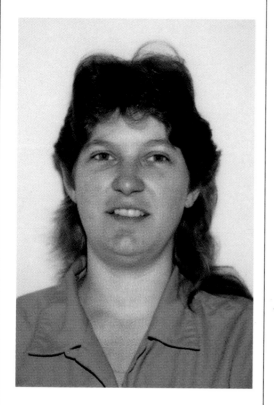

Dr. Julie M. Delger grew up in Gretna, Louisiana, a suburb of New Orleans. She obtained her Doctor of Veterinary Medicine degree from Louisiana State University in 1990. After a one-year Small Animal Rotating Internship at Auburn University in Alabama, she completed a two-year Dermatology Residency at North Carolina State University in Raleigh, NC. In August 1993 she successfully completed the American College of Veterinary Dermatology Board Certification Examination. In November 1993 she started full-time private practice at the SC Dermatology Referral Service in Columbia, SC. Her practice is limited to diseases of animal skin. All patients are referred by a family veterinarian.

Environmental Causes of Skin Problems

By Julie Delger, DVM
Diplomate, American College of Veterinary Dermatology
South Carolina Dermatology Referral Service
124 Stonemark Lane
Columbia, South Carolina 29210

INTRODUCTION

The skin is an amazing organ. It is the largest organ of the body and serves more functions than you might think. In addition to covering the body and protecting it from infection and contamination, the skin is also involved in regulating body temperature and keeping body and blood fluids inside where they belong. Other equally important but less apparent functions are touch sensation and the production of vitamin D.

Cats are exposed every day, just as people are, to environmental factors and substances that may cause skin problems. Whether or not the damage is permanent depends on the factor and how long the cat has been exposed. Skin thickness is also important, and you might be surprised to learn that cat skin is much thinner than human skin.

Most skin problems having an environmental cause are not linked to age, breed or sex of the cat. As you might suspect, exposure is the primary clue. In general, areas of the body where the skin is the thinnest are most susceptible to environmental damage. These areas include the ear flaps (called the pinnae), the abdomen and inner thighs, and the skin between the toes. This is just a general guideline, and there are many exceptions. In all cases, the goal must be to stop the exposure so the problem can be relieved. Prompt veterinary care is critical in treating and reversing the damage done to the skin, if reversal is indeed possible.

Specific diseases will not be discussed in-depth; rather, larger categories or classes of disease will be presented, with individual conditions mentioned when appropriate.

SOLAR DAMAGE

Sunburn

Sunburn is seen in virtually all domestic animals and man. As in humans, cats with less skin pigmentation (white or pink skin) are more susceptible to damage from the sun. Many may be entirely white. Cats of any age may be affected, although older cats are more likely to have problems. This is because the effects of solar damage, which are due to ultraviolet radiation, are cumulative. That means that it is repeated exposure over periods of time that are most likely to cause problems.

Ultraviolet light can cause permanent changes in the genetic makeup of the skin cells, as well as altering the structure of skin collagen and elastic fibers. These fibers are responsible for normal skin elasticity and texture.

Clinical signs (symptoms) of sunburn include reddened, tender or painful skin in those areas which have been exposed to the sun. Parts of the body most likely to be sunburned are the pinnae (ear flaps), abdomen, inner thighs, and the relatively hairless area between the eye and ear. If sun exposure is discontinued, these damaged areas may

resolve and heal on their own with no major consequences. If, however, exposure is persistent and prolonged, the reddened areas may progress to blistered, ulcerated areas which may be quite painful or pruritic (itchy). Large yellowish or bloody crusts may be seen as the ulcers attempt to heal. The skin may become thickened in these areas, which also represents an attempt at healing.

It is best to seek veterinary attention before the lesions become ulcerated; however, once this has happened, prompt veterinary care is essential to prevent progression of the disease to an irreversible point. In any case, sun avoidance is required and is a good preventive measure which should be taken with any cat which has a predomi-

Redness and hair loss caused by excessive solar exposure.

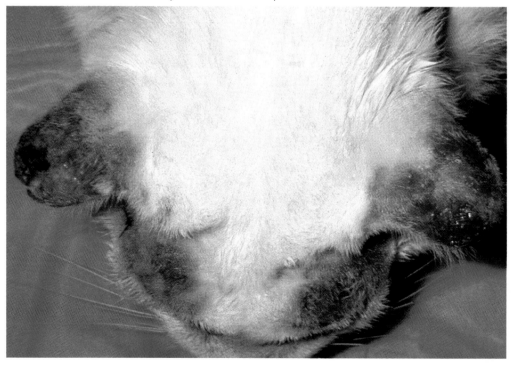

Cats are exposed to a variety of environmental factors and substances that can cause skin problems. This is especially true of those cats that are allowed to roam freely outdoors. Photo by Isabelle Francais.

nantly white coat or any cat excessively fond of sunbathing. If outdoor exposure is necessary during peak daylight hours, susceptible skin is best treated with sunscreens (SPF 15 or greater) before the cats go outside.

Skin Cancers and Sun Exposure

Most people are aware that sun exposure can cause skin cancers in people, and the same is true of cats. In addition to changing the structure of the skin, ultraviolet light also causes a decrease in the numbers of skin cells responsible for detecting and eliminating abnormal or neoplastic (cancerous) cells. This is why prolonged sun exposure predisposes cats (and people) to skin cancer.

Several types of cancer can be induced by ultraviolet light. The most common of these by far is called squamous-cell carcinoma, but other types exist. Most kinds of skin cancer are relatively slow-growing and can invade nearby areas although they are slow to spread to other parts of the body. Thus, with very early detection, a partial to complete cure may be possible.

Skin cancer most often arises at sites which have been subjected to chronic sun exposure, with or without previous sunburn. These body parts are the same ones most prone to sunburn—the pinnae (ear flaps), abdomen, and inner thighs. Cats with light-colored noses may develop these types of cancers on their noses also. Once the skin has become ulcerated, continued ultraviolet irradiation can alter the genetic structure of the

Redness of the area between the eye and ear associated with squamous-cell carcinoma.

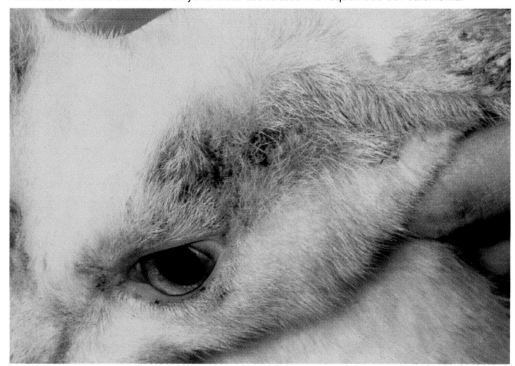

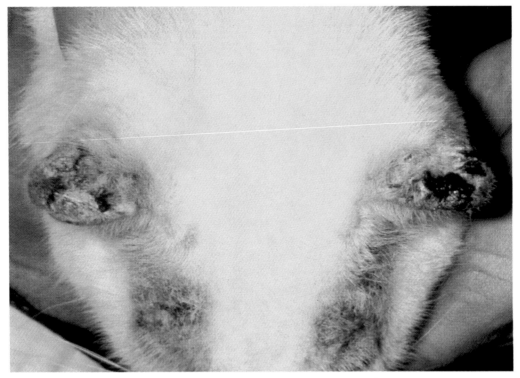

Extensive damage to the head and ears caused by squamous-cell carcinoma.

skin cells trying to heal the wound, which can lead to development of cancer. Skin cancers can also develop on non-sun-exposed skin if there is a problem with the immune system, such that abnormal cells are not recognized and removed.

The appearance of sun-induced skin cancers is variable. Some tumors are simply reddened, angry-looking raised lesions, while others are barely noticeable. These latter types may simply be reddened areas with blackish crusts, and they may or may not be painful or itchy. In most cases, there is some degree of hair loss in the affected area. Once the problem has progressed to this stage, your veterinarian will need to be consulted and

biopsies (pieces of the affected area) taken to confirm his or her clinical suspicion of cancer. Again, if detected very early, there is a reasonable chance for at least prolonged remission of disease, if not a cure. Like other forms of cancer, skin cancer can be fatal if left untreated.

Autoimmune Diseases and Sun Exposure

While solar exposure and ultraviolet radiation do not cause this type of disease, almost all forms of autoimmune disease are made worse by sun exposure. The most obvious examples are systemic lupus erythematosus and its more benign counterpart, discoid lupus erythematosus. Most autoimmune skin diseases

Discoloration of the skin around the nail bed seen in a case of squamous-cell carcinoma.

A non-genetic but still troubling sensitivity to sunlight (photosensitivity) can be seen in some cats receiving certain prescription drugs. Just as in people, some medications cause individuals to be sensitive to sunlight and to develop rashes with sun exposure. Even though this type of drug reaction is rare, owners should be aware and react promptly if the situation arises.

target sensitive skin areas, and the damage done makes the skin more susceptible to solar damage. Then, the sun can cause additional damage, as described above. This also makes the autoimmune disease more clinically resistant to proper therapy. Any cat which has been diagnosed as having an autoimmune skin disease should be kept out of the sun, especially between 10 a.m. and 4 p.m. Sunscreens are necessary for cats that need to be outdoors during peak daylight hours. Once again, sun exposure doesn't cause autoimmune skin disease, but it may be a complicating factor.

MISCELLANEOUS CONDITIONS

In rare instances, cats may have genetic defects which lead to the deposition of substances in the skin that react to sun exposure. The result is that exposure to sunlight causes severe damage to the skin. Fortunately, these types of genetic problems are rare in cats, as they are in people.

Frostbite

One of the functions of the skin is to maintain normal and consistent body temperature. This is achieved by sweating (evaporation of moisture from the skin) in warm weather and by limiting the amount of blood that circulates to the skin (constriction of the small blood vessels in the skin) during cold weather. Of course, cats also regulate their body temperature by panting. When the temperature is very low for prolonged periods of time, the small blood vessels in the skin remain constricted. If those vessels constrict long enough, the skin dies from lack of circulation. We call this reaction "frostbite."

Cats of any age, breed, or sex can get frostbite. Temperatures do not need to reach freezing to cause frostbite although this is most often what happens. Other parts of the body that can be affected are those that tend to have poor circulation. These include the pinnae (ear flaps), nose, tail tip, scrotum, and toes. The appearance of frostbite lesions varies with its duration. When warmed, the affected areas will often appear very red and may be quite painful. If the area is not warmed, then it will eventually appear purple-black and will usually be painless since the nerves in the skin have also died. Often the skin just adjacent to the blackened, dead skin will be very red and painful.

Your veterinarian should be consulted immediately when frostbite occurs. As with most health problems, the sooner this is done the better the outcome is likely to be.

Burns

Burns may be caused by increased temperature, by caustic or corrosive chemicals, or by radiation. The appearance is similar for all of these causes, in most cases, and all ages, breeds and genders are susceptible. Thermal burns may be due to hot liquids contacting the skin, by direct contact with hot solids (such as space heaters, radiators, heating pads, etc.), or by prolonged exposure to heated air, as with hair dryers or heat lamps. Heat causes skin damage by altering the physical structure of the individual cells, actually cooking the skin. The hair may be singed, but this does not happen in all cases. Areas of the body most often affected are the abdomen, back, and sides.

At first, the skin is red and painful. As the lesions age, de-

pending on the severity of the burn, blisters may form. Since cats' skin is so thin, blisters are not always seen. Ulcers and weeping, or oozing of serum through the skin follow the blister stage. The hair over these areas often becomes matted down to the skin. The skin, which is now dead, will slough off to leave large ulcers which ooze blood, serum and sometimes pus. When large areas are burned, the cat's ability to maintain a normal temperature is impaired. Massive amounts of fluid can be lost through the ulcerated areas, leading to dehydration. The raw areas are also prime colonization sites for bacteria, which can easily gain access to the bloodstream and cause severe illness or death.

Many chemicals are caustic and corrosive, and will literally digest the skin upon contact. The appearance is usually identical to those of thermal burns. If exposure to any corrosive or caustic chemical occurs, the skin should be rinsed immediately with cool water and your veterinarian should be consulted.

Because of the potentially devastating after-effects of burns, any burn must be treated promptly by your veterinarian. Quick care may save your pet's life and a lot of money in medical bills.

Contact Dermatitis

Contact irritation differs from chemical burns in that the offending substance, rather than killing the skin cells outright, causes inflammation of the skin. The list of substances capable of causing such a reaction is exhaustive and includes salt on roadways, cleaning solvents, flea collars, shampoos, garden sprays, and plants. In many ways the reaction resembles an allergy but there are some important differences. With contact irritation, exposure to the substances causes irritation in the skin and inflammation. Without prompt recognition and treatment, the skin can become darker in affected areas as the inflammation persists.

Parts of the body most affected by contact irritation depend upon the specific irritant compound. For instance, irritation of the chin, lips, and nose may be due to plastic resins in a food dish, while irritation caused by a carpet deodorizer will cause inflammation on the paws and abdomen.

Early cases of contact irritation may appear as red areas which the cat licks, chews, rubs, or scratches, although the problem may not be itchy at all. These areas may then become thickened, hairless, and may gain (hyperpigment) or lose (hypopigment) skin coloration. When contact irritation is suspected, your veterinarian will question you about possible irritants in the home. Try to prepare a short list before consultation with him or her. Think about shampoos, cleansers, carpet cleaners, disinfectants, insecticides (or any other potentially dangerous household chemicals) or plants to which your pet may have been exposed.

Bites and Stings

Bites and stings can be very variable in their appearance and diagnosis is not always easy. In some cases the bites just cause irritation, while in other cases there may also be an allergic component. Cats most likely to be bitten or stung tend to be young, curious cats and breed doesn't seem to be a factor. Body parts usually affected are the face, paws, and abdomen, although any site may be injured. In some cats kept outdoors, the ear tips may be attacked by biting flies, causing crusting and hair loss. Usually, the most common problem seen with bites and stings is a red bump or pimple, or sometimes a small welt. These may or may not be itchy. Most will resolve without treatment in 2-7 days if no more bites occur. In the case of some types of spiders, these inflamed areas may progress to areas of dead, blackened skin with subsequent ulceration, or to areas of intense inflammation and swelling, which may then become ulcerated.

In those cats that have allergic reactions to bites or stings, the reaction is a little more intense. Hives may be seen and are generally considered a mild form of allergic reaction, but they may also be the first sign of a much more serious condition called anaphylaxis, or anaphylactic shock. Anaphylaxis can be fatal; therefore, any animal showing hives should be taken immediately to a veterinarian for treatment.

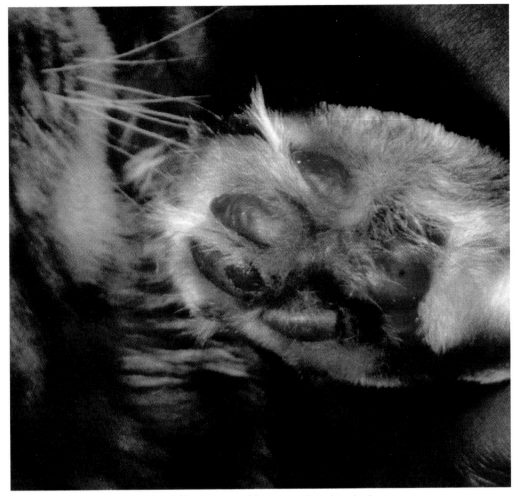

Ulceration of the foot pad caused by contact with a corrosive chemical.

Snakebite

Any kind of snake may cause skin damage by biting a cat, even if it is not poisonous (venomous). Snakes' mouths are full of bacteria, which become implanted in and under the skin when a bite occurs. Again, as with insect and spider bites and stings, young, curious cats as well as hunting cats are most likely to be snakebitten. The face and legs are most commonly bitten. A variably painful, swollen lump may result, which may progress to an abscess or ulcer.

In cases of bites by venomous snakes, the affected area quickly becomes quite red and painful, and extremely swollen. When the face or head becomes swollen, one must be concerned about the cat's ability to breathe, as the swelling is often internal as well as external. The reason for the intense swelling is damage to blood vessels caused by the venom itself. If the swelling involves a leg, the blood supply to the entire limb may be compromised, resulting in a sort of gangrene. Some venoms contain a toxin which damages the nervous system and can be fatal.

Snakebite is one of the most pressing medical emergencies. Do not wait for serious problems to occur if you know your cat has been bitten—seek veterinary care immediately!

Skin-Fold Dermatitis

In cats with excessive folding of the skin upon itself, such as Persians and Himalayans, the facial folds can trap moisture and tears and create a favorable environment for the growth of bacteria and yeasts. Any age cat of either sex may be affected. The inner part of the fold is reddened and moist, and is usually hairless. Sometimes pus is present, and a foul odor is common. Occasionally, red bumps or crusts are seen.

Generally, keeping the folds clean and dry is all the care required for treatment and prevention. Wiping the area several times a day with peroxide or salt water is usually sufficient. If bumps are seen, the problem should be treated by a veterinarian because the skin is likely infected. In severe cases, surgery may be needed. Again, consult your veterinarian for his or her advice regarding your pet.

Foreign Body Reactions

The major function of the immune system is to detect and eliminate invaders of the body. However, the process is often much more successful for bacte-ria and viruses than for large particles such as thorns, the sharp tips of some grasses (awns), burrs, pins, needles, or other foreign bodies. The skin of the paws and face are most commonly involved, but foreign bodies may also get lodged in the eyes, ears, mouth, nose, and body cavities. Any age, breed, or sex can be affected. Often, the foreign body goes undetected, especially if it is small, until the immune system has responded to its presence by mounting an inflammatory attack. Some signs which may be typical of foreign body reactions include swollen, red bumps, with or without pus, hair loss from the cat's persistent licking, and sometimes lameness. Owners are often shocked to learn that a grass awn lodged in the paw can make its way under the skin surface for quite a distance, often tracking bacterial infection in its wake.

Foreign bodies often carry bacteria and hairs, which are also seen as foreign by the immune system, into the tissues, further complicating the situation. A deep-seated infection may ensue, the severity of which depends upon the type of bacteria involved. A veterinarian should be consulted at the earliest detection of a suspected foreign body, or as soon as exposure to potential foreign bodies is verified.

Trauma

Trauma is very common and can afflict any age, breed, or sex of cat. Any part of the body may be injured, although the paws and legs are more commonly hurt. A traumatic wound may be nothing more than a scratch, or it may be a deep laceration, abrasion, or complete tearing away of the skin from the underlying tissues (called a degloving injury). The latter are quite painful. In winter, cats can climb onto the warm engine of a car, and suffer injury when the car is started and they get caught in a fan belt. This type of injury is more common than you might imagine, and very serious.

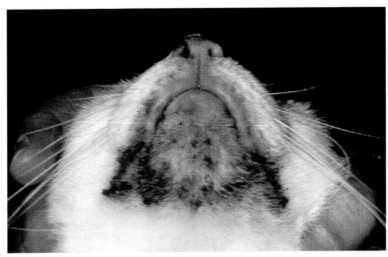

Redness and crusting of the lips and chin of a cat, typical of contact irritation caused by resins in plastic food dishes.

While simple first aid may be all that is required for most small scratches and abrasions, any wound that extends through the full thickness of the skin should be seen by a veterinarian as soon as possible.

Myiasis (Fly Strike)

Undoubtedly one of the most abhorrent conditions seen by veterinarians, fly-strike is caused by some species of flies depositing eggs in and near open wounds. The result is the presence of fly larvae (maggots) in the wound. This condition can occur whenever there is injured skin and exposure to flies. Even very small wounds may become infested. A special kind of myia-sis is caused by the burrowing of a type of fly larva (*Cuterebra*) into the skin of cats, usually around the head and neck. The fly larvae are in the soil around the openings of rodent burrows, and the cat becomes infected when investigating the hole. The lesion caused by these larvae is usually seen as a small hole in the skin with some clear fluid draining from it. Occasionally, the "worm" can be seen moving inside of the hole.

If larvae are seen in any wound, the cat should be taken as soon as possible to a veterinarian for removal of the larvae and for wound cleaning and disinfection.

ADDITIONAL READING:

Ackerman, L.: *Pet Skin and Haircoat Problems.* Veterinary Learnings Systems, Trenton, New Jersey, 1993, 216pp.

Muller, G.H.; Kirk, R.W.; Scott, D.W.: *Small Animal Dermatology.* W.B. Saunders, Co., Philadelphia, 1989, 1007pp.

Dr. Phyllis Ciekot got her Bachelor of Arts degree from the College of Notre Dame of Maryland in 1985 and veterinary medical degree from Ohio State University in 1989. She completed an internship in small animal medicine and surgery at North Carolina State University and went on to complete a residency program in Small Animal Oncology (and a Master's degree in Veterinary Clinical Sciences) at Colorado State University. Dr. Ciekot then became board-certified in the specialty field of veterinary medical oncology and is a cancer specialist for animals. Dr. Ciekot practices her specialty at her office in Scottsdale, Arizona.

Lumps and Bumps

By Phyllis Ciekot, DVM
Diplomate, American College of Veterinary Internal Medicine (Oncology)
Sonora Veterinary Surgery & Oncology
6969 E. Shea Blvd., Suite 200
Scottsdale, Arizona

INTRODUCTION

Pet owners can easily recognize skin abnormalities in their companions, which explains why skin cancer is usually diagnosed earlier than tumors located in other organ systems. Tumors (synonyms are neoplasm, cancerous growth) are abnormal tissue masses that arise by proliferation of the body's own cells. Today's constantly expanding knowledge and skill in the practice of veterinary medicine, improved nutrition and the use of vaccines have resulted in an increased life span for feline companions.

The skin is the second most common site of neoplastic disease in the cat, with an incidence rate of about 84 tumors per 100,000 cats per year. Although the occurrence of tumors in the skin of cats is much lower than that of the dog, it has been observed that skin tumors in the cat are more likely to be malignant. The overall incidence for feline skin tumors reveals no significant breed or sex predilections, although Siamese cats have a significantly lower risk for skin tumors than do other breeds. White cats, particularly those living in geographic regions with increased sun exposure and/or higher altitudes, have an increased risk for squamous-cell carcinoma. Tumors can appear during all periods of an animal's life; however, the median age for cats with skin tumors is 12 years.

Contributory causes of skin tumors have been recognized in the cat, particularly solar radiation and specific viruses. Lack of skin pigmentation in white cats exposed to sunlight, particularly around the eyelids, ears and nose, is a definitive predisposing factor to squamous-cell carcinoma. The chance of this tumor arising in these regions in white cats is 13 times that of cats with pigmented skin. Another type of tumor, fibrosarcoma, is thought to occur in young cats infected with the feline sarcoma virus. This tumor recently has also been associated with vaccine reactions in cats.

CLASSIFICATION OF SKIN TUMORS

The first step in the clinical assessment of a skin mass by the veterinarian is to differentiate neoplastic tissue from non-neoplastic masses such as an abscess. If the diagnosis is a cancerous growth, the clinician will then attempt to distinguish whether the mass is benign or malignant in nature. In general, malignant neoplasms are characterized by sudden onset, rapid enlargement, ulceration, invasion into surrounding tissues and spread to distant sites (metastases). Another important consideration highly suggestive of malignancy is the tendency of the tumor to regrow at the original site after surgical removal. Neoplasms are classified as malignant based on certain microscopic criteria.

Tissue from a tumor can be sampled in a variety of ways depending on the location and the size of the neoplasm. Fine needle aspiration biopsy and excisional biopsy are the most frequently used methods.

The prognosis partially depends on the microscopic appearance of the cells taken from the tumor described under the microscope. Tumors are "graded" based on the structure and degree of maturation of the cells observed. In general, well-differentiated, mature-appearing tumors have a better outcome than undifferentiated, immature-appearing tumors. Tumor size, location, involvement of lymph nodes and evidence of metastasis (spread) to other body organs define the "stage" of the neoplasm. Blood tests, radiographs (x-rays) and other diagnostic tests may be performed by the veterinarian to determine the extent of the process. If the tumor is confined to the original area of occurrence, the overall outlook is more favorable. Cancer which has been found to be spreading to distant areas of the body, such as the lymph nodes or lungs, has a more guarded prognosis.

GENERAL METHODS OF TREATMENT

The type of therapy recommended for a skin tumor will depend upon the tumor type, size, location, the local or distant spread (metastases) determined to be present and the overall health of the patient. For some tumors, no treatment may be the most appropriate decision, particularly when dealing with obviously benign tumors in geriatric patients. In such cases, the risks of treatment exceed the risk associated with the tumor if left untreated.

As the majority of skin tumors in the cat are malignant, treatment should be sought as early as possible. Therapeutic efforts include surgery, radiation therapy, chemotherapy (medical therapy) and cryosurgery (freezing). More recent innovative treatments include photodynamic therapy, immunotherapy and hyperthermia (heat therapy). The science of veterinary oncology is a constantly expanding field, and new treatments are constantly evaluated for many tumor types.

COMMON SKIN TUMORS OF THE CAT

Cutaneous neoplasms are classified according to their tissue of origin: epithelial tumors, tumors of melanin-producing cells and mesenchymal (soft tissue) tumors. Epithelial tumors of the skin include basal-cell tumors, squamous-cell carcinoma, papillomas, sebaceous-gland tumors, sweat-gland tumors, and tumors of the hair follicles. Of the mesenchymal-origin tumors, fibrosarcoma is the most important. Other tumor types include mast cell tumors, lymphosarcomas, mela-

A tissue biopsy of a tumor is the definitive method to obtain a diagnosis.

nomas, and hemangiomas. In addition to neoplasms, other mass lesions that occur in cats are benign cysts, abscesses, and granulomas of bacterial, fungal and immunologic origin.

EPITHELIAL TUMORS

Basal-cell tumors (basal-cell carcinoma, basal-cell epithelioma)

These are the most common feline skin tumors. They can develop on any part of the body, but commonly occur on the head, neck and shoulders. Usually solitary, these tumors are frequently heavily pigmented, raised and ulcerated. Metastasis (spread) of basal-cell tumors in the cat is extremely rare.

Surgical excision is the best therapy for this cancer. Radiation therapy has also been utilized suc-cessfully. Recurrence of the tumor after excision is rare.

Squamous-cell carcinoma

This is the second most common skin tumor in the cat. Solar radiation, nonpigmented skin, high altitude and possibly genetics are thought to predispose cats to this tumor. These are usually ulcerated masses which either can be cauliflower-like or crater-like with irregular borders. More than 75 percent of these tumors occur on the head, usually on the ears, nose, eyelids and face.

This cancer is typically highly invasive but late to metastasize to distant locations. Some research has correlated the microscopic characteristics of the tumor (poorly differentiated) with the tendency to spread to other sites and recur.

Treatment for squamous-cell carcinoma includes various combinations of surgery, cryosurgery (removing tissue by applying very cold substances such as liquid nitrogen or liquid carbon dioxide), radiation and chemotherapy. Prompt surgical removal of lesions can be curative, especially in easily accessible sites such as the tip of the ear. Recent studies also indicate that hyperthermia (therapy using high temperatures) may also be an effective treatment alternative.

Papillomas (warts)

Papillomas are rare in cats. They can be solitary or multiple, well delineated, cauliflower-like and usually are small (less than 0.5cm) in size. The face, eyelids and limbs, particularly of older cats, are most frequently affected. Treatment consists of surgical excision.

Sebaceous-gland tumors

These are uncommon in cats. Older cats are most often affected and these neoplasms can occur at any site on the body. Usually solitary, these are typically diagnosed as adenomas, or benign glandular tumors. Sweat-gland tumors are even more rare, yet also occur in older cats and can occur at any location. Adenocarcinomas are most frequently diagnosed. Early surgical excision is the treatment of choice for both types, but the prognosis is more guarded for sweat gland adenocarcinomas.

Tumors of the hair follicles (Trichoepitheliomas and pilomatrixomas)

These are rare benign skin tumors in the cat. They can occur at any location on the body. Surgical excision is the treatment of choice.

CONNECTIVE TISSUE (MESENCHYMAL) TUMORS

Fibrosarcoma

Fibrosarcomas are tumors which occur in adult to aged cats and can affect any part of the body. Solitary, nodular and irregular in shape, these neoplasms are firm and variable in size and consistency. Local invasion into surrounding tissues is the hallmark of these tumors and this makes complete surgical excision difficult in some locations. Some studies suggest that these tumors can metastasize frequently to other areas, and other research contradicts these findings. A consistent factor related to this tumor's aggressive behavior, however, is its appearance microscopically (i.e., the more undifferentiated and immature in appearance, the worse the prognosis).

Radical surgical excision is the treatment of choice for this tumor. A wide area of normal-appearing tissue around the tumor should be removed to ensure complete excision. Radiation therapy, hyperthermia and chemotherapy are other treatment options which may be required for adequate control of tumor growth. Prognosis is always guarded for this tumor due to its high tendency to regrow at the original site of removal.

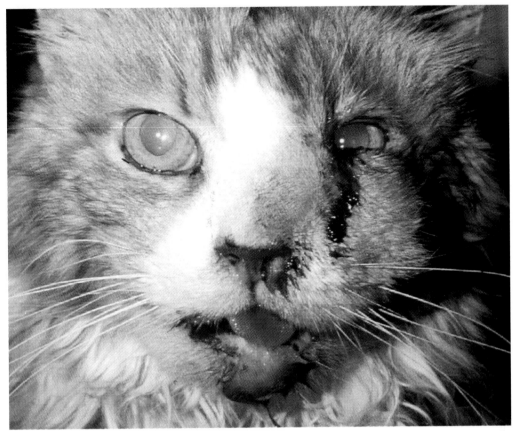

Squamous-cell carcinoma on the face of a lightly pigmented cat. These tumors are frequently ulcerated and bleed easily when manipulated.

Some feline fibrosarcomas are virally induced by the feline sarcoma virus (FeSV), particularly in very young cats. This viral infection has also been associated with feline leukemia virus (FeLV) infection. These tumors are usually multiple, located in any area of the body and are usually not responsive to treatment. These tumors are distinctly different than the solitary fibrosarcomas found in older cats and have a much poorer prognosis for treatment.

Hemangiomas

Hemangiomas are rare skin tumors usually occurring in aged cats. Solitary in nature, bluish-red in color and well delineated, these lesions are more common in the trunk, neck and limbs. Complete surgical excision is curative. Another more rapidly growing malignant form of this tumor is a hemangiosarcoma. Again, surgical removal is the treatment of choice for this type, but recurrence at the site of removal can be common.

OTHER TUMOR TYPES

Mast-Cell Tumor (mastocytoma)

Mast-cell tumor is a skin tumor which can occur in any breed, but seems to be more common in older male cats. Mastocytomas can occur anywhere on the body, but especially can occur on the head, neck and limbs. These tumors can be solitary or multiple, raised, firm, well demarcated and ulcerated. Some cats may also be itchy at the site of tumor location. Most feline mast-cell tumors appear to be benign, but some may be more aggressive and spread to lymph nodes, liver and spleen fairly quickly. Unlike dogs, cats rarely develop gastrointestinal ulcers or bleeding tendencies in conjunction with this tumor.

Treatment of solitary mast-cell tumor is surgical removal. Radiation therapy and chemotherapy appear to be promising alternatives for mast-cell tumors in multiple sites, but more research is necessary.

Lymphoma (lymphosarcoma)

This is a rare skin cancer of aged cats. These tumors are extremely variable in appearance, but can be solitary or multiple, raised or flat, reddened or blanched in color and are usually itchy. Unfortunately, this disease is inevitably fatal (usually within a few months), but chemotherapy has been successful in prolonging survival and quality of life for a short time.

Melanoma (melanocytoma)

These are rare in cats, usually occurring in aged individuals. The neoplasms are solitary, brown to black in color, variable in size and well delineated. Metastasis to distant sites is common, with usually two/thirds of reported feline cutaneous melanomas spreading to lymph nodes and lungs. Early radical surgical excision is the therapy of choice, but the prognosis is poor.

Multiple mast-cell tumors on the inside of the hind leg of a cat. Note the red, ulcerated appearance of these tumors.

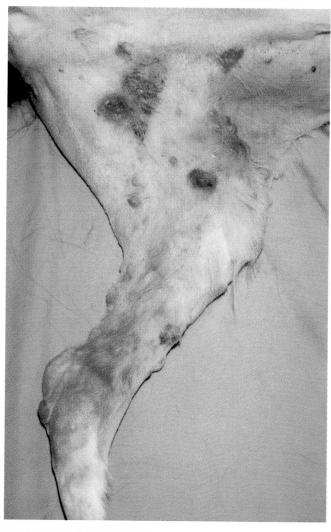

Cysts (epidermoid, dermoid)

Cysts are uncommon in the cat but are benign, well delineated, firm masses that can occur at any location on the body. Sometimes they are filled with a yellow oily fluid or brown-gray greasy material. Cysts can readily become infected, particularly with self trauma. Typically these cysts are located on the neck and trunk and are found in middle aged to older cats. Do not attempt to squeeze and evacuate a cyst; these lesions can rupture into the underlying skin layers and cause painful inflammation to occur. The treatment of choice is surgical removal.

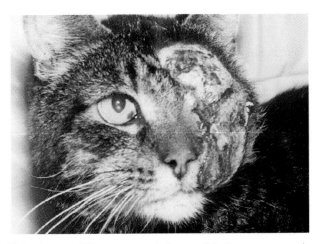

This ulcerated fibrosarcoma is impossible to remove surgically because of its location on the face and its large size. It is important to have your cat examined as soon as possible when a rapidly changing skin lesion develops so that treatment can be instituted early.

SUMMARY

Oncology is the medical specialty dealing with cancers. Now, more than ever, there are new methods of diagnosis and treatment that can help pets who are afflicted with cancer. Each type of cancer has its own biological behavior and anticipated response to different therapies. Your veterinarian can provide you with additional information and, if necessary, a referral to a veterinary cancer specialist, an oncologist.

ADDITIONAL READING

Barton C.L.: Cytologic Diagnosis of Cutaneous Neoplasia, An Algorithmic Approach, *Compendium of Small Animal Education*, 1987; 9(1):: 20-33.

Macy, D.W., Reynolds, H.A.: The Incidence, Characteristics and Clinical Management of Skin Tumors of Cats. *Journal of the American Animal Hospital Association*, 1981; 17(6): 10261033.

Moriello, K.A.: Rosenthal R.C., Clinical Approach to Tumors of the Skin and Subcutaneous Tissues, Veterinary Clinics of North America, *Small Animal Practice*, 1990; 20(4): 11631190.

Strafuss, A.C.: Skin Tumors. Veterinary Clinics of North America, *Small Animal Practice*, 1985; 15(3): 473488.

Susanek, S.J., Withrow, S.J.: Tumors of the Skin and Subcutaneous Tissues. In *Clinical Veterinary Oncology*, Withrow and MacEwen, E.G., editors, J.B. Lippincott, Philadelphia 1989.

Theilen, G.H., Madewell, B.R.: Tumors of the Skin and Subcutaneous Tissues. In *Veterinary Cancer Medicine*, Theilen and Madewell, editors, Lea and Febiger, Philadelphia, 1979, pp. 123-191.

Dr. Alexander Werner graduated from the University of Pennsylvania School of Veterinary Medicine, followed by an internship at the California Animal Hospital in Los Angeles, California. He completed a residency in veterinary dermatology at the University of California, Davis, School of Veterinary Medicine, where he met his wife Bonnie. Dr. Alexander Werner is a Diplomate of the American College of Veterinary Dermatology.

Dr. Bonnie Werner graduated from the University of California, Davis, School of Veterinary Medicine, followed by an internship at the Coast Pet Clinic in Hermosa Beach, California. She completed a residency in small animal internal medicine at the Louisiana State University School of Veterinary Medicine. Dr. Bonnie Werner is a Diplomate of the American College of Veterinary Internal Medicine. Both Drs. Werner live in Southern California, where they practice together in a referral specialty clinic.

Zoonotic Conditions

By Alexander H. Werner, VMD, Diplomate, ACVD
and Bonnie E. Werner, DVM, Diplomate, ACVIM
Animal Dermatology Centers
Valley Veterinary Specialty Services
13125 Ventura Boulevard
Studio City, CA 91604

INTRODUCTION

The dictionary definition of a zoonosis is a disease which can be directly transmitted from animal to human. In this strict sense, there are few skin-related zoonotic diseases. However, if a more liberal definition is adopted, as in diseases that can involve animals transmitting a disease to humans, several important conditions can be included. Cats have been particularly (and perhaps excessively) implicated as a cause of human disease. Dermatophytosis (ringworm), papular urticaria (flea bite dermatitis), *Cheyletiella* and *Notoedres* infestation, Sporotrichosis, *Rochalimaea henselae* infection (cat scratch disease), and *Yersinia pestis* infection (bubonic plaque), are the most common feline zoonoses. As most of these diseases are discussed elsewhere in this text, this chapter emphasizes typical human lesions and methods aimed at reducing the likelihood of transmission. Whenever these diseases are suspected or diagnosed, it is imperative that both human and veterinary dermatologists be involved in the treatment of their respective patient species.

DERMATOPHYTOSIS (RINGWORM)

Human infection with dermatophyte species that normally affect animals has been reported as a common zoonosis. Dermatophytosis, often referred to as "ringworm" because of its circular presentation in humans, is caused by fungal organisms that colonize the hair and upper skin layers. Of the several fungal organisms (dermatophytes) that cause dermatophytosis, *Microsporum canis* is most often associated with cat-to-human transmission. *Microsporum canis* is a zoophilic dermatophyte, meaning that it has become adapted to animals and is rarely found in soil. Dermatophytes can be isolated from normal (asymptomatic) cats and dogs as well as animals with visible signs of disease. Long-haired cats are frequently asymptomatic carriers; one report found infection in over one third of long-haired show cats. Human infections may occur in more than half of households with infected cats, therefore, the zoonotic potential of feline dermatophytosis cannot be overemphasized.

The classic human ringworm

lesion is an inflamed, slowly expanding circle of redness and scaling. A central healing region may occur. Lesions are frequently itchy, and scratching may result in scarring. In haired regions, the hair shafts break as they weaken from fungal infection and circular areas of hair loss result. The most commonly affected areas for human dermatophytosis of feline origin are covered areas with increased moisture (such as beneath watch bands and jewelry), and regions frequently in contact with infected cats (such as the face and forearms). In general, the young, the elderly, and the ill or immunosuppressed individual are most at risk due to their decreased resistance. Dermatophytic lesions typically resolve after several weeks, with or

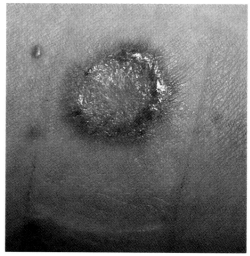

Circular, reddened, and scaling lesion of human dermatophytosis.

without therapy. Permanent scarring and deeper, severe infection can occur; therefore consultation with a human dermatologist is always warranted.

Circular, scaling lesion of feline dermatophytosis (ringworm).

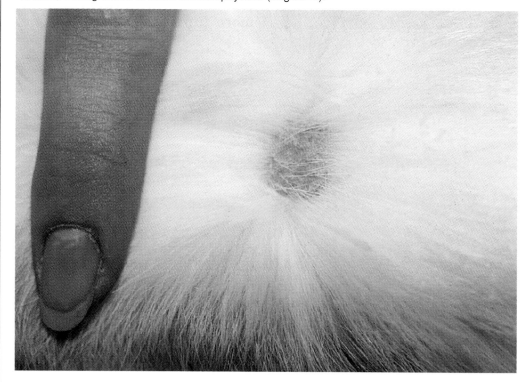

Transmission of ringworm from cat to human may occur by direct contact with infected cats (symptomatic or asymptomatic), or by contact with fungal spores in the cat's environment. Spores can persist for up to several years. Therefore disinfecting the

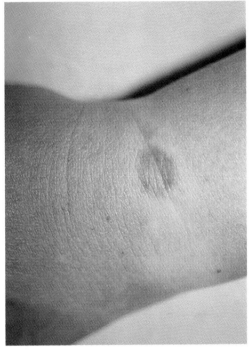

Human dermatophytosis lesion in the region of a watchband.

environment is important in the overall treatment of dermatophytosis. Unfortunately, research into the effectiveness of environmental treatments has yielded poor results for the methods most often recommended. Topical treatment of all cats, systemic treatments when necessary, and disinfecting the home should all be utilized for maximal effectiveness.

Recently, a new ringworm vaccine for cats that are already infected with *Microsporum canis* has been released for use in the United States. Initial studies of this vaccine indicate that while the severity of lesions and the clinical appearance of vaccinated cats improves more rapidly than non-vaccinated cats, there is no reduction or shortening in the number or period of time that fungal organisms are shed into the environment. Therefore, while a vaccinated cat may appear to heal faster, the potential for zoonotic infection remains the same. In addition, the vaccine manufacturer indicates a short period of efficacy (two weeks) even after multiple booster injections. Unlike most vaccines, it is not intended as a preventative treatment for the disease. Only diligent treatment of cats and repetitive fungal cultures (until no more fungal organisms are detected) can decrease the chance of cat to human transmission.

PAPULAR URTICARIA (FLEA BITE DERMATITIS)

Flea bite dermatitis is an extremely common skin disease of cats, and the most common flea affecting humans is *Ctenocephalides felis*, the cat flea. Fleas are poorly host-specific – this means that they will bite almost any passing animal. As a general rule, fleas prefer to feed on their animal hosts, so if humans in the household are being bitten often, the number of fleas in the house is probably so high that there are not enough animals to feed on. Some animals and people are particularly attractive to insects, including fleas, and may be bitten more frequently. Similarly, some people are allergic to flea bites and have more severe reactions, rather than just developing irritated bites. The largest numbers of human flea bites occur in environments with many animals, especially in temperate climates where fleas flourish throughout the year. The major concern with human flea bites, besides the itching, is the rare possibility that fleas may spread diseases such as typhus, cat scratch disease, plague, and tularemia from cats to humans.

Typical lesions of flea bite dermatitis in humans are clusters of itchy, red, raised bumps on the feet and ankles (hence the name, papular urticaria). Flea bites may occur in characteristic groups of three, sometimes referred to as "breakfast, lunch and dinner," although this appearance has rarely been recognized by the authors. Insect bites tend to occur in regions that are most exposed to the specific insect. Flea bites may be distinguished from the bites of cat mites because they tend to occur on the feet (which are nearest the floor where fleas hatch) and the bites of cat mites tend to occur in areas most in contact with the cat (mites live exclusively on the cat).

Successful treatment and prevention of flea bite dermatitis requires adequate flea control.

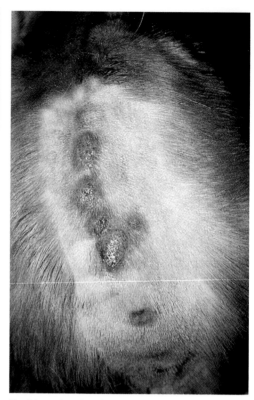

Reddened, raised, and itchy lesions of feline flea allergy dermatitis.

The itchiness associated with most flea bites may take several days to subside, even after fleas are removed from the house.

CHEYLETIELLA AND NOTOEDRES MITE INFESTATION

Cheyletiella blakei is a large mite that infests the haircoat of cats. Because of its large size, infested cats appear to have "moving dandruff." Although cats may not always show obvious signs of discomfort or itchiness, humans in contact with infested cats commonly develop itchy red rashes on the arms, face and chest. Many reports have implicated this mite as the cause of significant human disease, with up to 20% of exposed humans developing lesions. Cheyletiellosis is less frequent in areas where fleas are controlled because the mite is highly sensitive to routine insecticides. When people have itchy skin lesions for which no obvious cause can be found, human dermatologists are urged to consider the possibility of *Cheyletiella* infestation in their patients' cats. These animals should be referred to a veterinary dermatologist for examination.

Notoedres cati is an uncommon sarcoptid-type mite of cats. Unlike *Cheyletiella*, in which infested cats may appear normal, cats with *Notoedres* are always extremely itchy. A characteristic "mantle" of adherent crusts and scabs will develop, and the cats will often lose weight and body condition due to their excessive scratching. *Notoedres* infestation occurs commonly in specific geographic locations within the North America, but can be seen sporadically in other areas.

Human lesions of *Notoedres cati* bites are also itchy. Lesions most often develop on the arms and chest—areas in contact with infested cats. Red, inflamed, and highly itchy bumps develop in these areas. The astute veterinarian should carefully question the owner of an itchy animal to determine if any humans in the household have itchy bites. Occasionally, *Notoedres* infestation in a cat can be diagnosed before any lesions develop, simply because the owner complains of

Reddened, self-traumatized lesions of human flea allergic dermatitis.

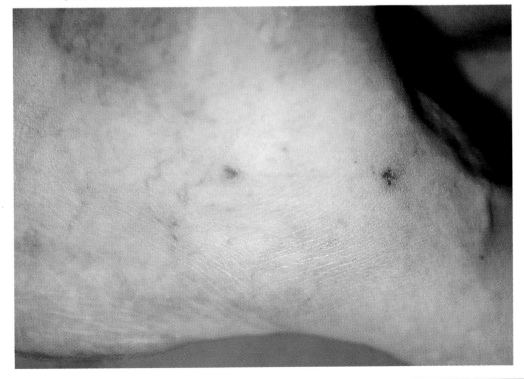

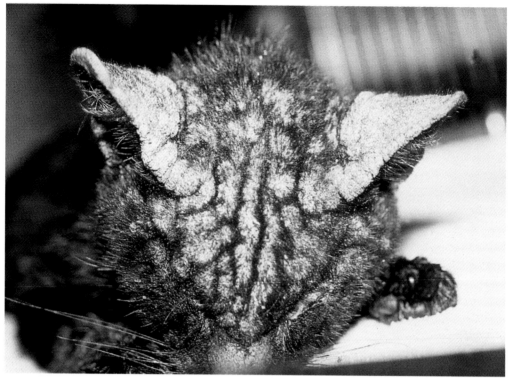

Extreme scaling and crusting on the ears and head with feline Notoedric mange.

being itchy after petting the cat.

Therapy for human cases of *Notoedres* and *Cheyletiella* bites depends upon adequate treatment of the affected cat. Because both *Cheyletiella* and *Notoedres* can only live on the cat, the corresponding human lesions will quickly resolve once the cat is treated.

SPOROTRICHOSIS

Sporothrix schenckii is a fungus that lives in decaying vegetation and soil. Human and animal disease most often occurs when abraded or cut skin is exposed to infected debris. Sporotrichosis in humans has been called "rose-gardener's disease" because of its propensity to occur after the skin is pricked

by a rose thorn. In South America, human cases of sporotrichosis are usually associated with armadillo hunting because the fungus grows in armadillo dens and hunters often are wounded during attempts to dislodge the animals. Cats also develop lesions following contamination of wounds. In general, direct transmission of Sporothrix organisms from animals to humans is rare because the number of organisms in infected lesions is very low. The cat, however, is the exception to this rule because large numbers of Sporothrix organisms can be found within the exudate and tissues of infected feline patients. These feline organisms also seem unusually infective. There are

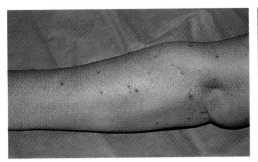

Multiple small, reddened, and itchy lesions of human Notoedric mite bites.

lung and other organ infections, are rare. However, because of the possibility of severe (possibly fatal) disease, sporotrichosis must be considered a serious zoonotic hazard.

Unlike the previously mentioned diseases, in which treatment of the affected cat is a very helpful part of treating any human lesions, people with sporotrichosis must be treated

many reports of cat-to-human sporotrichosis transmission in the medical literature, but only a few involving other animal species.

In humans, both skin and non-skin forms of disease occur, although the skin and lymph node variety occurs in 80% of - cases. Characteristically, a single nodule develops on the hand or arm, which then opens and drains fluid. Lesions often are painless unless associated with a secondary bacterial infection. The generalized forms of sporotrichosis, including

Raised, ulcerated, and weeping lesions of feline sporotrichosis. Slide courtesy of Christina Hutson, DVM, Redondo Beach, California.

Closer view of the above photo. Note the scabbing of lesions from self-trauma.

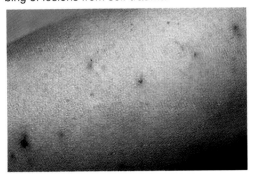

for extended periods of time with antifungal medications. Extreme caution must be exercised when treating infected cats. Feline-transmitted human sporotrichosis has developed in areas associated with cat scratches or bites, in sites of previous injuries, and in non-injured skin. Fungal organisms have reportedly penetrated skin and caused disease at the edge of gloves worn to protect humans against infection. Thus, strict hygienic and isolation protocols must be adhered to when treating infected cats. Fortunately, recent advances in antifungal medications, including new, highly effective drugs against sporotrichosis, have improved the prognosis for infected animals and humans. Therefore it is much less acceptable now to consider euthanizing infected cats.

ROCHALIMAEA HENSELAE INFECTION (CAT SCRATCH DISEASE)

Cat scratch disease has long been considered an obscure disease of questionable cause. Also known as "cat scratch fever," the disease has recently resurfaced, and there is new evidence indicating the true cause of this human illness. It is important to remember that the cats themselves are simply carriers and do not actually acquire the disease.

Cat scratch disease is common, with yearly human cases in the United States exceeding 22,000. In up to 90 percent of cases there is an associated history of a cat—especially a kitten—scratch or bite wound. It may be the most common cause of chronic, benign lymph node enlargement in children. Recent evidence has implicated the rick-

Reddened plaque-like lesions of sporotrichosis on a human chest. This condition occurred as a result of contact with the household cat (pictured with its lesions). Slide courtesy of Christina Hutson, DVM, Redondo Beach, California.

ettsial organism *Rochalimaea henselae* as the causative agent of cat scratch disease; classification of this organism is still in dispute, and occasional cases may be caused by the organism *Afipia felis*. *Rochalimaea henselae* has also been implicated as the cause of more severe diseases.

In one report, all of the cats in households with cat scratch disease had *Rochalimaea henselae* organisms cultured from their blood, although none of these cats showed any signs of disease. In addition, 41 percent of cats from a local shelter had this organism cultured from their blood. Cultures of *Rochalimaea henselae* were also obtained from the fleas on these animals. Considering the fact that there are fifty-seven million cats residing in one-third of all United States households, there is great potential risk for human exposure to the *Rochalimaea* organism.

Transmission of cat scratch disease is believed to result from exposure through bites, scratches, and oral or respiratory secretions. According to a recent study, infection in cats occurs most often in kittens under one year of age, during which time they shed organisms into the environment. This would seem to be the most likely reason for the frequent implication of kitten scratches as the source of human infection. An insect vector, most likely fleas, may also be involved. Not all cases of cat scratch disease have been corre-

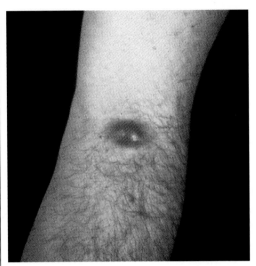

Raised, reddened nodule of human sporotrichosis. Slide courtesy of Victor Newcomer, MD, Santa Monica, California.

lated with cat-produced traumata (although 99% of cases in one study reported prior contact with a cat). Infection from the environment or from contact with a carrier cat followed by touching a mucous membrane (mouth or eyes) is possible, though considered unlikely.

Although children under twenty-one years of age make up 80% of cases, a large number of adults become infected. A seasonal incidence (primarily colder months) has been reported. Most cases are benign and self-limiting. Fever, malaise, and an inflamed nodule at the site of inoculation is common within two weeks of a cat-associated injury. Enlargement of a local lymph node, with rare drainage, occurs. Lesions and swollen lymph nodes usually regress within six weeks; however, persistent cases can occur. Immunocompromised individuals, and up to 2% of immunocompetent individuals, can develop complications, including fatal vascular and nervous system disease. Cat scratch disease is considered by some experts to be a human immunodeficiency virus-related disease. Diagnosis is primarily based on the exclusion of other causes of enlarged lymph nodes, a positive cat scratch skin test, and a recent cat-associated injury near the initial lesion. Serologic testing (blood test) is also currently available. Treatment is generally ineffective and therefore rarely attempted, although antibiotics are administered in severe cases (such as the severe manifestation known as bacillary angiomatosis). Immunity following infection is believed to be lifelong.

Considering the vast number of cats that appear to be asymptomatic carriers of *Rochalimaea henselae*, the statistical possibility for human transmission is high. The plausibility of either avoiding all cats, or eradicating the organism from the pet cat population, is poor. To assist in reducing potential human disease, routine veterinary-directed flea control programs should be instituted, and all cat-associated bite wounds or scratches should immediately be washed with an antiseptic soap.

YERSINIA PESTIS INFECTION (BUBONIC PLAGUE)

Plague is a severe, sometimes fatal, infection caused by the bacterium *Yersinia pestis*. This disease is most often discussed from a historical perspective as the deadly "Black Death" or "Black Plague". However, new cases of plague are still diagnosed every year in both humans and animals.

Plague is maintained in nature in wild rodent populations as a flea-rodent (enzootic) cycle, which serves as a constant reservoir. In general, wild rodents are resistant to the disease. Infection periodically moves from its natural reservoir to non-resistant animals, such as ground squirrels and prairie dogs, resulting in large population "die-offs." When these populations are depleted, their fleas seek alternate food sources, increasing the potential for human and cat exposure. Dog and cat fleas are less likely to transmit plague to humans than are rodent fleas. However, roaming cats can increase the risk of human exposure to plague by bringing wild rodents and fleas into the human environment. Surveillance of wild rodent populations and their predators (e.g. coyotes) can help predict when domestic animal and human infections are likely to occur. Rodent "die-offs" are of particular importance.

Clinical infection is similar in humans and cats, with three recognized syndromes. The most common form, bubonic plague, causes fever, malaise and enlarged and painful lymph nodes which may open and drain fluid. Draining lymph nodes are called "buboes," hence the name. Cats

A cat that roams outdoors is far more likely to develop parasitical diseases than is the cat that is kept indoors. Photo by Robert Pearcy.

often have high fevers and draining lymph nodes around the head and neck, probably caused by inoculation of the oral cavity (mouth) following ingestion of an infected rodent. Enlarged lymph nodes may also develop in the region of flea bites. Disease can spread, resulting in generalized illness (septicemic form), or can occur suddenly as a severe, sometimes fatal pneumonia (pneumonic form).

In the United States, most human cases are reported in the rural areas of the Southwest. These areas are considered "plague-enzootic" because of the constant presence of *Yersinia pestis* infection in the wild rodent population. During the past fifty years, 362 human plague cases have been diagnosed in the United States. Thirty-two cases of human plague were reported in California between 1962 and 1992, with seven fatalities. In 1993, ten cases of human plague in the United States were reported; in the first quarter of 1994, one case of human plague was confirmed. Transmission from cats to humans occurs from flea bites or from contact with infectious discharges. The importance of this latter route of human exposure is becoming clear and may especially produce severe pneumonic disease. Twenty-five percent of reported cat-associated cases of human plague have involved veterinarians and their staff, due to increased exposure to sick cats.

The diagnosis of bubonic plague is confirmed by culturing *Yersinia pestis*, or by specialized fluorescent antibody testing of exudate and serum. Infected cats are readily treatable; however, extreme caution must be taken to avoid transmission to humans (by both infectious discharges and fleas) during treatment. Routinely using flea control products on pets, preventing contact between cats and wild rodent populations, and reducing wild rodent populations in human environments can reduce the incidence of cat to human transmission.

SUMMARY

The role cats play in transmitting diseases to humans varies from common (dermatophytosis and flea bite dermatitis) to uncommon (notoedric mange and cheyletiellosis) to rare (sporotrichosis, cat scratch disease, and plague). Although the potential for some serious human disease exists, this rarely necessitates removing the pet from the household, even when a transmissible disease has been confirmed. The benefits of having a pet are well documented and far outweigh the risks involved with feline companionship. Common sense, safe animal handling techniques, adequate flea control programs, and thorough wound cleansing can dramatically reduce the incidence of human disease. If a human is suspected of having a disease that could have been transmitted from his cats, consultation with a veterinary dermatologist or internist is strongly recommended.

ADDITIONAL READING

Adal KA, Cockerell C.J., Petri W.A. Jr. Cat scratch disease, bacillary angiomatosis, and other infections due to *Rochalimaea*.. *New England Journal of Medicine*, 1994; 330(21): 1509-1515.

Eidson M., Thilsted J.P., Rollag O.J.. Clinical, clinicopharmacologic, and pathologic features of plague in cats: 119 cases (1977-1988). *Journal of the American Veterinary Medical Association*, 1991; 199(9): 1191-7.

Fitzpatrick T.B., Eisen A.Z., Wolff K., Freedberg I.M., Austen K.F., editors. *Dermatology in General Medicine*. Third edition. McGraw-Hill Book Company, 1987. Chapters 178, 181, 195 and 208

Greene C.E., editor. *Infectious Diseases of the Dog and Cat*. W.B. Saunders Company, 1990. Chapters 59, 61, 64 and 69.

Muller G.H., Kirk R.W., Scott D.W. *Small Animal Dermatology*. Fourth edition. W.B. Saunders Company, 1989. Chapters 5, 6, 7, and 8.

Cats are notorious for their meticulous grooming habits. However, a cat that grooms itself to excess—to the point where its skin is irritated—may require veterinary attention. Photo by Isabelle Francais.

Dr. Patricia White received her Doctor of Veterinary Medicine degree from Tuskegee Uniiversity's School of Veterinary Medicine in 1983, then pursued and completed a small animal internship at Michigan State University in 1984. She then returned to Tuskegee where she served on the faculty for three years. Dr. White then completed a dermatology residency program at the Ohio State University as well as a Master of Science degree. A board-certified veterinary dermatologist, Dr. White currently operates the Atlanta Veterinary Skin and Allergy Clinic, which she founded in 1992.

Understanding Medications

By Patricia White, DVM
Diplomate, American College of Veterinary Dermatology
Atlanta Veterinary Skin & Allergy Clinic, P.C.
33 Avondale Plaza North
Avondale Estates, Georgia

INTRODUCTION

As pet owners, we take on a huge responsibility when caring for our dependent friends. When an injury or illness occurs, we employ our knowledge of first aid to encourage the healing process, or we seek the advice of a veterinarian. Most people have at least one over-the-counter (OTC) oral analgesic (aspirin, ibuprofen, etc.), and one topical anti-itch or antibacterial cream or lotion in the medicine cabinet. Whether a home remedy or a prescription drug, it is important to know and understand some basic concepts of classes of medications, how they work, and when they should be used or avoided.

HORMONAL THERAPY

Glucocorticoids

Cortisol is an extremely potent hormone, is vital to normal bodily functions and affects every cell in the body. It is required for carbohydrate, protein, and fat metabolism, influences water and sodium balance, and affects glucose synthesis. Normal (physiologic) amounts of cortisol are made by the adrenal gland located in the abdomen next to the kidney. The amount of cortisol made by the adrenal gland is held in delicate balance by the release of a hormone called ACTH. ACTH comes from a gland in the brain called the pituitary gland. The ACTH hormone stimulates the adrenal gland to make more cortisol when blood levels drop below a predetermined level, then a "feedback process" tells the pituitary gland to stop making ACTH when cortisol is back to normal. Administration of cortisone for therapeutic purposes can upset this delicate balance and will adversely affect immune function, normal tissue metabolism, and may suppress both adrenal and pituitary gland function. The impact brought about by a single dose may continue for weeks to months.

Synthetic glucocorticoid (corticosteroid) hormones, also referred to as steroids, cortisone, prednisone, or allergy shots/ pills, are the most common group of drugs prescribed for pruritic (itching) skin conditions. They are also the most used and abused class of drug in dermatology. The medication may be injected, administered orally, or applied topically. The effect on the body is related to the amount given, the potency of the drug, and how long the effects last. Short-acting cortisone (hydrocortisone, prednisone, prednisolone) is prescribed to reduce itching, redness, and swelling. It is invaluable in treating hypersensitivity reactions (flea allergy, pollen allergies), "hot spots", and to relieve the discomfort in areas of self-inflicted trauma. Longer-act-

ing more potent steroid medications (triamcinolone, dexamethasone) suppress different parts of the immune system and are a vital part of therapy in diseases such as lupus erythematosus and cancer.

Problems can occur when these powerful drugs are given indiscriminately. Increased water intake, increased frequency of urination, increased appetite, aggressive behavior, and weight gain are common side effects of even short term cortisone therapy. Evidence of cortisone excess includes the development of fat deposits over the lower back, a pot-bellied appearance to the abdomen, decreased tolerance to exercise, and panting.

Profound thinning of the skin in a cat treated with an injectable corticosteroid (Depo medrol®).

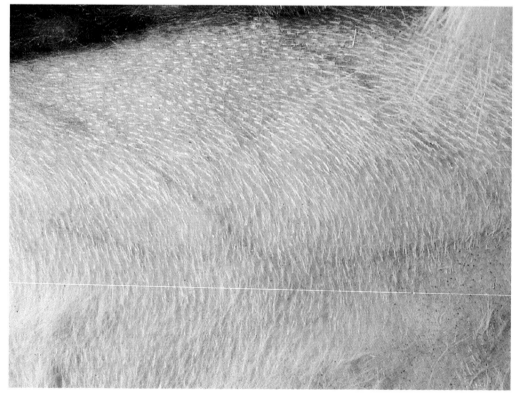

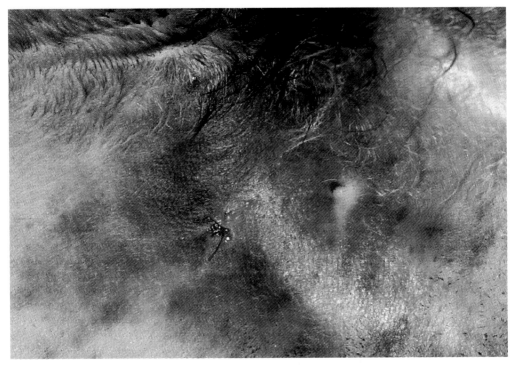

Bruising of the skin associated with the use of an injectable corticosteroid.

Dermatologic changes associated with cortisone excess include hair loss, thin skin, development of comedones (blackheads) on poorly haired skin, and the development of bruising in areas of minor trauma. Systemic effects of cortisone excess may include stomach ulcers, pancreatitis, and diabetes.

Most people understand that excessive amounts of cortisone can cause severe damage to tissues and the immune system. A guide to using cortisone safely is to be sure that the smallest dose of the weakest formulation possible is given as infrequently as possible to bring about the desired effect. Anti-inflammatory doses are administered daily for five to seven days, then the dose is reduced to every other day. Alternate day therapy allows adrenal gland activity to continue uninterrupted and insures the availability of physiologic cortisone if needed.

Progestational Compounds

Megestrol acetate (e.g., Ovaban) is a potent long-acting progestational drug that was once used abundantly to treat a variety of skin problems in cats, including miliary dermatitis, eosinophilic granuloma, and conditions involving symmetrical hair loss. Its physiologic effects are numerous and relatively non-specific. Today there are diagnostic methods available to identify the specific cause of these skin reactions allowing selection

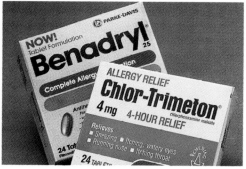

Diphenhydramine (Benadryl®) and chlorpheniramine (Chlor-Trimeton®) are two commonly used antihistamines that are available without a prescription. Chlorpheniramine is the preferred product to use in cats. Diphenhydramine has been associated with unwanted side effects in the cat.

of therapy that is specific in activity. Therefore, there is little need for progestational drugs in feline medicine unless other specific treatments have been tried and have failed. The side effects seen with even short term use warrant due caution whenever the drug is given. Side effects include increased appetite and thirst, weight gain, aggressive or submissive behavior, mammary gland tumors, transient diabetes mellitus, and pyometra (infected uterus).

ANTIHISTAMINES

Glucocorticoids are very effective in controlling itch, but the side effects associated with prolonged use have prompted the evaluation of other safer drugs to control itch. Antihistamines are a group of drugs that have proven to be quite helpful, especially in controlling signs of atopy (inhalant allergy, hay fever). Antihistamines are H-1 blockers. This means that

they reduce itching by preventing histamine, a promoter of inflammation, from attaching to specific histamine receptors present on inflammatory cells. Although the antihistaminic effects play a role in the animal's response, these drugs also cause drowsiness (sedation). It is the sedative effects that can be especially beneficial to the chronically itchy pet because it allows the pet (and owner) to rest.

There are seven classes of antihistamines; many are available only with a prescription. Individuals respond to antihistamines differently, so a therapeutic two-week course of two different drugs will allow selection of one that will work the best on your pet. One OTC antihistamine that is safe for cats is chlorpheniramine maleate (Chlortrimeton—one 4mg tablet per 10-pound cat every 12 hours). Diphenhydramine (Benadryl) is available OTC but should not be used because it may cause bizarre behavior in cats. Antihistamines rarely eliminate pruritus (itchiness) entirely, but most allow a marked reduction in the amount of cortisone needed to control itching. Occasionally, antihistamines will cause an increase in itching, trembling, excitation, and marked sedation. Discontinuing the drug will eliminate these adverse effects. Antihistamines have been associated with birth defects in dogs; until the connection in cats is better understood, it is best that they not be used in breeding queens.

FATTY ACID NUTRITIONAL SUPPLEMENTS

Linoleic acid and arachidonic acid are polyunsaturated fatty acids that are essential components of healthy skin. When these key elements are lacking in the diet, the hair coat becomes dull and the skin dry and scaly. Luckily, the source of these essential fatty acids is vegetable oil. One teaspoon of safflower oil added to the diet daily often will correct the problem.

Fatty acids also play a fundamental role in the formation of prostaglandins and leukotrienes during periods of inflammation. Eicosapentaenoic acid (EPA—derived from marine fish oil) and gammalinolenic acid (GLA—derived from evening primrose oil or borage oil) are specific dietary fatty acids that have been shown to reduce inflammatory prostaglandins and leukotrienes. These fatty acids have been proven effective in reducing pruritus and dermatitis in allergic pets. In addition, when fatty acids are combined with an antihistamine, glucocorticoids often can be eliminated from the treatment regime.

NON-STEROIDAL ANTI-INFLAMMATORY DRUGS (NSAIDS)

This group of drugs covers a wide range of pharmacologically diverse compounds. Most NSAIDs are available OTC, and many are hidden in topical and oral medications. It is important for an owner to read all drug labels, to know which NSAIDs are safe to use, and recognize signs indicating toxicity.

NSAIDs are present in both OTC and prescription drugs, and are used to reduce inflammation and swelling caused by prostaglandins and thromboxanes. Prostaglandins and thromboxanes are chemicals made by tissues after an injury, infection, or adverse immunologic reaction. Their presence in tissue contributes to the pain, redness, and swelling experienced at the site of an injury.

Aspirin is the most commonly used anti-inflammatory drug (next to cortisone) in companion animal medicine. In dogs, it is used to relieve muscle and joint pain, to help with vascular (blood vessel) complications following treatment for heartworm disease, and may also reduce pain and swelling associated with chronic self trauma (licking, chewing, biting). Aspirin is rarely used for treating dermatologic problems in cats. Cats are very sensitive to the toxic effects of aspirin because they lack a specific liver enzyme (glucoronyl transferase) needed to break down and eliminate the drug from the body. Aspirin is the *only* NSAID that can be given to cats but should not be administered without the supervision of a veterinarian. The recommended dose is 10-20 mg/kg (1/2 baby aspirin per 10-pound cat) and should not be administered more frequently than every other day. Toxic side effects include depression, inappetence, vomiting, GI bleed-

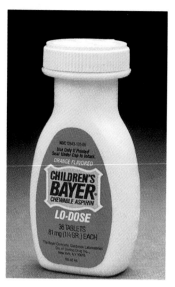

Buffered aspirin is the *only* non-steroidal anti-inflammatory agent (NSAID) that can be safely used in cats. Check with your veterinarian before use to make sure it can be safely given to your cat.

consequence, accidental overdoses are a possibility for pets as well.

There is a very narrow margin of safety between therapeutic and toxic or lethal doses, and none of these drugs should be used on your pet without specific veterinary supervision. Most of these drugs require glucuronide conjugation by the liver, an enzyme in short supply among cats. These drugs therefore should *never* be given to cats. Toxic side effects include increased heart rate, difficulty breathing, vomiting, urinary retention, lethargy, hyperactivity, seizures, and coma. The most life-threatening side effect is an irregular heart beat leading to cardiac arrest.

ing, bone marrow depression, anemia and liver and kidney failure.

Ibuprofen, naproxen, and acetaminophen should never be used in cats. Toxic side effects with these drugs include kidney damage, GI upset and bleeding, liver damage, decreased clotting of blood, bleeding tendencies and anemia.

PSYCHOTHERAPEUTIC MEDICATIONS

A lot of public attention has been given to the use of several human antidepressant drugs such as amitriptyline HCl (Elavil®) and Fluoxetine HCl (Prozac®). Due to the popularity of these kinds of drugs, they have become the number one cause of drug overdose in humans. As a

TOPICAL MEDICATIONS

General Principles

The skin is a protective barrier between internal structures and the environment. The outer layers of skin, called the stratum corneum, together with the hair coat and oily glandular secretions, provide a carefully balanced physical, chemical and immunologic defense against all sorts of worldly microbes and toxins. When the skin is washed or when medications are applied, some of the protective oils and secretions are removed along with these pathogens.

Most early skin problems are characterized as red, swollen, and warm to the touch; this is the classic description for inflammation. An acute lesion such as a hot spot will also be moist to the touch. Topical therapy is directed at reducing all of these signs. The formulation of medication (lotion, cream, ointment, etc.) can be as important to the efficacy of therapy as the actual drug because the form may determine how rapidly and efficiently the medication can traverse the outside defenses in order to be absorbed.

Lotions are the mildest formulation in that they tend to be water-based liquids in which medications have been suspended. The liquid phase will evaporate after application leaving behind a thin film of the active ingredient to be absorbed into the skin. Lotions are non-occlusive, non-oily, somewhat drying, and the best form for moist lesions. Calamine lotion is a classic example of a lotion.

Creams and ointments usually contain some mixture of oil, water, and the suspended medication. Creams are a little heavier than lotions, may have an oil base, may take longer to be absorbed, but stay on the skin longer than lotions. They are excellent for softening mild crusting lesions. When applied after cleaning a wound, they can create an oil barrier between the skin and outside world. The effect is to extend the time the medication is in contact with the

Acute moist dermatitis, also known as a "hot spot." This is not a specific diagnosis but is a common sequel to flea hypersensitivity, allergies, and other skin afflictions.

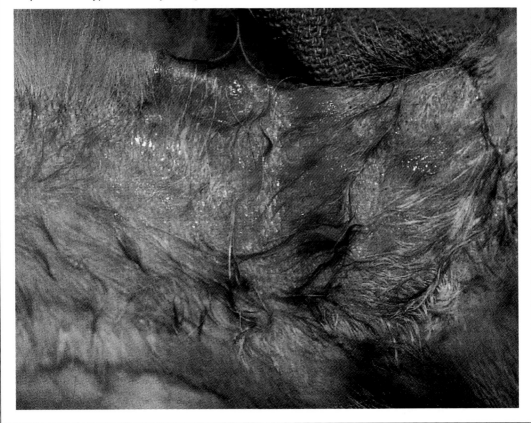

One of the advantages of topical medications is ease of application. Photo by Isabelle Francais.

skin. Ointments are heavy, tend to stay on even when water is applied, and are occlusive by nature. The best example of an ointment is petrolatum, or Vaseline®. Ointments should not be used on hot spots but are excellent for conditions where the skin is thickened and hard.

Occasionally, one or more ingredients in topical creams or lotions can cause an allergic or irritant contact dermatitis. This is evident by increased redness, swelling, scaling, blistering, or itching after applying the product. Should this happen, discontinue use and wash the area with fresh water and a mild soap to remove the medication.

The Medications

For the most part, topical medications (creams, ointments, and lotions) have limited use on our pets because they tend to lick every bit off as soon as it is applied. This point is an important one because seemingly harmless topical preparations may be quite dangerous if ingested. Fortunately, a large amount of the medication must be ingested for most drugs to be toxic. It is important to know which items in our own medicine chests are appropriate and safe to use on our pets. There are literally thousands of OTC topical medications with endless numbers of active and supposedly inert ingredients. Their advantages include ease of application, rapid response, and relative benign effects on the patient overall.

Most skin conditions causing

Hair balls are not uncommon in cats. There are preparations available that can help in the elimination of swallowed hair. Photo courtesy of Four Paws.

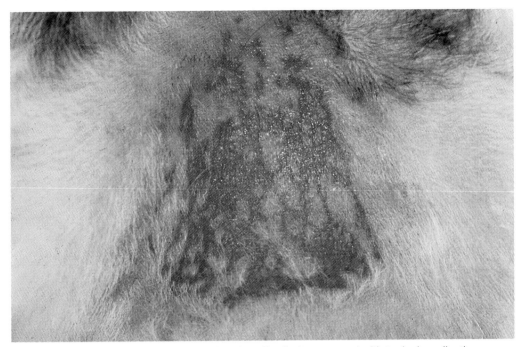

Acute moist dermatitis (hot spots) can often be effectively managed with topical medications.

itch are generalized. Home remedies in the form of soothing soaks (colloidal oatmeal) and rinses are available and will provide temporary relief until you can get to the vet's office. A 10-15 minute soak in cool water can be helpful. The cooling effect competitively inhibits itch, providing temporary relief that may last for 1-2 hours. If the itching is due to a dry skin condition, then oils or humectants added to the water will help alleviate the dryness. The addition of colloidal oatmeal (Aveeno—Rydell Laboratories; Episoothe—Allerderm/Virbac) to the water may extend the soothing and anti-itch effects for several hours to 1-2 days.

Aluminum acetate powder (Domeboro®—Miles Pharmaceuticals) added to water is an as-tringent, helps dry moist lesions, and reduces itching for several hours to 1-2 days. It is especially effective for hot spots, areas that the pet has made raw by excessive licking, and moist inflamed ear conditions. It has no antimicrobial effects so the area should be gently cleansed first. One packet of powder is mixed in 1 pint of cool water, and the solution is applied as a compress for 10 minutes twice daily for 3-4 days. Once the affected area is dried, it use may be discontinued.

Camphor (Campho-phenique) and menthol (Gold Bond Powder) are added to topical lotions and sprays because of their cooling effects. Topical anesthetics (lidocaine, benzocaine) and antihistamines (Benadryl, Caladryl) are also added to products and

Chin acne is common in cats. Benzoyl peroxide is often the treatment of choice because it helps clean out the follicles (pores).

may provide temporary relief to localized lesions. Zinc oxide and calamine are mild astringent, antipruritic products present in many topical OTC products.

Topical corticosteroids are available as creams, lotions, ointments, or sprays and are used abundantly for both human and veterinary dermatologic conditions. The reduction in redness and itching after application is dramatic and almost immediate, but significant amounts of the drug may be absorbed systemically when applied to inflamed skin. Hydrocortisone (0.5% or 1.0%) is the safest form and is available alone or in combination with antibiotics in numerous OTC products. More potent corticosteroids are available only with a prescription. Local side effects include aggravation of an existing infection and thinning of the skin. Systemic effects have been observed with long-term use and are the same as those described for excessive systemic use described above. You should use a cotton ball to apply the medication to minimize the possibility of absorbing the medications through your skin.

Benzoyl peroxide is a potent antimicrobial product that also has "follicular flushing", degreasing, and anti-itch properties. Benzoyl peroxide is present in many veterinary shampoos but is also available as a cream or gel for treatment of local lesions. As a cleaner, it is very effective in breaking down and removing dried tissue exudate and greasy glandular secretions. Its potent antimicrobial effects and ability to open plugged hair follicles make it the treatment of choice for chin and muzzle acne. The disadvantage of benzoyl peroxide is that it can be a potent skin irritant and may cause redness, swelling, and occasionally blisters if left on too long. It also may bleach the skin, hair coat, as well as fabric. There are several OTC products containing benzoyl peroxide, but the concentration (usually 10%) is too strong for our pet's skin. Veterinary products containing 3-5% benzoyl peroxide are safest and may be applied 1-2 times a day.

The most common OTC antibiotic products (Polysporin, Neosporin, Panalog) contain a combination of bacitracin, neomycin sulfate, and polymyxin B sulfate. If the pet leaves the application on long enough, then the medication will diffuse through the upper layers of skin. Occasionally, a contact allergic reaction is seen from these triple antibiotic medications and are attributed most frequently to the neomycin. An adverse reaction to the medication should be suspected if the wound improves for the first few days after the medication is applied, then suddenly gets worse.

Topical medications are best suited for small, localized lesions. The first rule of thumb when applying a topical medication is "if it is wet (e.g., hot spots, feline eosinophilic plaques) dry it, if it is dry (scaling disorders) rehydrate or moisten it. All wounds should be cleansed before using a topical medication to ensure that no dirt or bacteria is trapped under the medication. The more hydrated the skin is, the more rapidly the medication will diffuse into the skin. My preference in treating mildly infected superficial wounds is first to clip away any hair around the wound. The second step is to gently cleanse the skin with an antimicrobial cleanser (e.g., Phisoderm, Betadine). Thoroughly rinse and dry the area making sure that *all* the cleanser has been removed. Then apply a small amount of non-occluding antibacterial lotion or cream. These steps should

When selecting grooming products for your cat, be sure to choose those formulated for cats. Photo courtesy of Hagen.

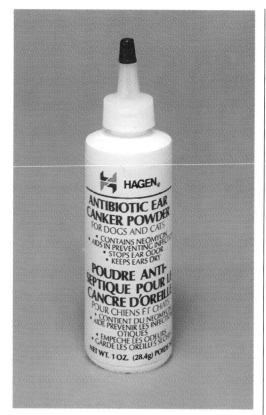

Infections of the external ear canal can be related to allergies and ear mite infestation. There are medications available to treat such infections. Photo courtesy of Hagen.

be repeated once to twice daily for 7-10 days. If the problem persists or worsens, seek the advice of a veterinarian.

EAR MEDICATIONS

Infections involving the external ear canal accompany allergic conditions and ear mite infestation in cats and can become chronic problems. There are endless numbers of ear medications, most designed for use in dogs. Most contain a combination of antifungal (miconozole or clotrimizole), antibacterial (neomycin, polymyxin), anti-inflammatory (hydrocortisone, tria-

mcinolone, or betamethasone), and parasiticidal (thiabendazole) drugs. Your veterinarian should examine the ear canal and ear drum before the medication is applied, since some antibiotics (gentamicin, neomycin) may cause hearing loss if the ear drum is ruptured. Like all chronic conditions, the cause of the ear problem should be identified specifically to maximize the potential for cure.

SUMMARY

Owners are confronted on a daily basis with information about medications. This chapter should help you to determine when a drug is warranted, the properties of that drug, and side effects that might be anticipated. Do not give any drug to your pet unless your veterinarian has approved its use and you fully understand the purpose for giving the drug and any adverse effects that might result.

ADDITIONAL READING

Ackerman, L.: *Pet Skin and Haircoat Problems.* Veterinary Learning Systems, Trenton New Jersey, 1994, 216pp.

Codner, E.C.; Thatcher, C.D.: Nutritional management of skin disease. *Compendium on Continuing Education for the Practicing Veterinarian*, 1993; 15(3): 411-423.

Rosser, E.J. Jr.: Antipruritic drugs. Veterinary Clinics of North America, *Small Animal Practice*, 1988; 18: 1093-1099.

Your cat does not have to be plagued by skin and haircoat problems. Your vet can prescribe a course of treatment that will help to provide relief. Photo by Isabelle Francais.

Dr. Jean Swingle Greek is a board-certified veterinary dermatologist practicing at the Dermatology & Allergy Clinic for animals in Overland Park, Kansas, just south of Kansas City. She divides her time between her practice, writing articles and lecturing. Dr. Greek graduated from the University of Wisconsin School of Veterinary Medicine, completed her internship at the University of Tennessee and her dermatology residency at the University of Pennsylvania.

Safe Use of Insecticides

By Jean S. Greek, DVM
Diplomate, American College of Veterinary Dermatology
Dermatology and Allergy Clinic
10333 Metcalf Avenue
Overland Park, KS 66212

INTRODUCTION

As pet owners, veterinarians, veterinary technicians and groomers, we are concerned with keeping our pets comfortable and parasite free. In most environments, this mandates that we will have to treat both our animals and our homes with parasite-killing substances, called parasiticides. The term parasiticide is preferred to insecticide when we are discussing chemicals that kill parasites other than insects, such as ticks and mites. The purpose of this chapter is to provide guidelines to help you do this safely for both you and your pet.

Safety is dependent on a combination of factors. The active ingredients, the carrier solution, the formulation and interaction of multiple ingredients all merge to determine the ultimate safety of these products. Difference in tolerance to ingredients is also important. Some pets may be sensitive to ingredients that are generally safe for other members of their species. Some of us are more bothered by certain ingredients as well.

Most of the emphasis of toxicology reports involves acute toxicity, and this information is usually well-established. Unfortunately for those of us who are likely to be exposed chronically, long-term effects are not as well understood. The potential of insecticides to cause cancer and birth defects has not been consistently evaluated. Therefore, it is mandatory that we minimize our exposure to these agents and we make every effort to use the least toxic products.

PRODUCT SELECTION

Polyborates

Tremendous strides in creating less toxic environmental treatments are being made. One of the most exciting is the use of inert substances such as polyborates for environmental control. These products have essentially no toxicity for people or their pets. In the government-mandated studies required of all insecticides, the toxicity proved to be less than the toxicity of table salt. The tiny particles are impregnated in the furniture and carpets and act as desiccants to fleas. That is, they cause the fleas' outer shells to be disrupted, and the fleas die from dehydration. Additionally, the flea larvae eat the substance and die. The other advantage to this tremendously effective product is that it only needed to be applied once yearly. The most widely used version of the product is distributed by Fleabusters™ as **Rx for Fleas**™ powder. This is an extremely safe product. I feel that it is the house treatment of choice for pet owners who have fish, exotic pets or small children. It is also appropriate for individuals who are concerned about the effects of traditional parasiticides on their health and on the planet. This product is so safe that animals and people need not leave the house during treatment. Some dust may be noticed during the application process and for up to three days afterward. Particularly sensitive individuals may find this irritating but it has not been reported to be a health hazard. This seems to be most noticeable in cases where the carpet fibers are short, such as Berber carpets. Long term studies conducted on the miners of borates, the basic ingredient, have not found any ill-effects on health or reproduction.

Numerous similar products are becoming available. They are available for over- the-counter sales and may be applied by the homeowner. The disadvantages of these over-the-counter products are that they have not yet undergone the rigorous safety testing performed on the Rx for Fleas™ product. Also, achieving penetration of the carpet fibers may be less effective when done by the nonprofessional, as they lack the applicator. In California, only the

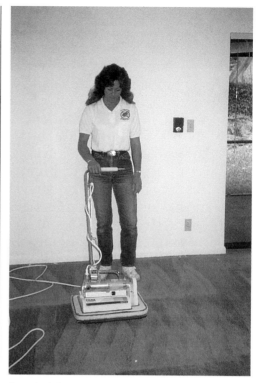

A technician applies Rx for Fleas powder™, a form of polyborate. Photo courtesy of Rx for fleas.

Rx for Fleas™ product is licensed. This is the only product that has met all the rigorous testing demands of that state. A disadvantage to all polyborate products is that they are inactivated when wet. Carpets cannot be steam-cleaned.

Insect Growth Regulators

Another important advance has been the development of insect growth regulators (IGRs). These products mimic naturally-occurring hormones in fleas. This prevents fleas from developing to the adult stage. These products are very low in toxicity, another way of saying they are extremely safe. They are available in products for both on-animal use and use in the inside environment. The toxicity of methoprene is extremely low. In some less-developed countries, it is routinely added to drinking water supplies to inhibit mosquitoes. The two IGRs currently available are fenoxycarb and methoprene. Fenoxycarb is the more stable of the two and may last in the environment for up to six months. Fenoxycarb has been formulated in products for outdoor use. Methoprene degrades in sun and therefore is not suitable for outdoor use. The increased stability of fenoxycarb allows you to treat the environment less frequently. Unfortunately, neither of these products kill adult fleas. Therefore, they must be combined with a more traditional adult flea-killing insecticide. Adulticides (parasiticides that kill the adult stage of the parasite) are, as a group, much more likely to be toxic. Adulticides combined with IGRs include chlorpyrifos, an organophosphate combined with fenoxycarb in Basus™ (Ciba-Geigy). Ovitrol™ (VetKem) contains methoprene combined with pyrethrins. The toxicity of these adulticidal insecticides is discussed below.

Microencapsulation

Another important advance leading to increased safety is a process know as microencapsulation. Insecticides are coated with a slowly-dissolving capsule made of polyurea. The capsule allows the insecticide to slowly permeate outward but is resistant to outside forces. The capsule slowly dissolves. Since the insecticide is delivered slowly and con-

sistently over a longer period of time, it not only lasts longer, but is also more safe. Duritrol™ (Merck Ag Vet) is a microencapsulated chlorpyrifos for indoor and outdoor use. Sectrol™ (Merck Ag Vet) is a microencapsulated pyrethrin spray for use on both pets and premises.

Beneficial Nematodes

Beneficial nematodes are naturally occurring worms. One type, *Steinernema carpocapsae*, is unique in that it feeds on only flea pupae and larvae. It is now being sold for outdoor flea control as Interrupt™ (Veterinary Products Laboratories) and Bio Flea Halt™ (Biosys). The product is applied with a tank or hose sprayer, and the worms die after all the flea larvae and pupae are eaten. Unfortunately, the worms may also die when temperatures drop too low or rise too high. They also require watering. This product is safe for animals and people.

Organophosphates and Carbamates

Organophosphates and carbamates are common small animal insecticides. The most common examples are fenthion, malathion, chlorpyrifos, diazinon and carbaryl. They are available in dips, sprays, powders, collars and foggers. Fenthion is sold as Pro-Spot™ (Haver) for spot-on use in dogs. Most cases of pesticide poisonings in both humans and animals are caused by this group of compounds. One study in California found that 50% of groomers using organophosphate dips had experienced some symptoms. Neither of these classes of compounds should be used in cats.

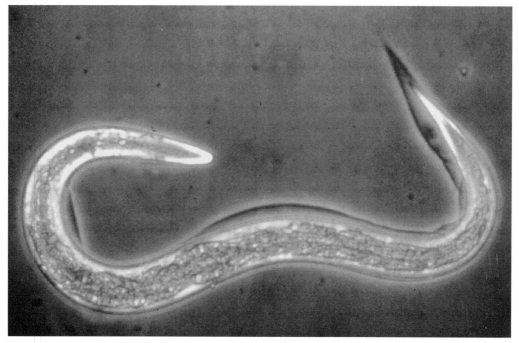

The beneficial nematode *Steinernema carpocapsae* is an active ingredient in the product Interrupt™. Photo courtesy of Biosys.

Kittens have died from exposure to flea collars containing dichlorvos. Cats have also become ill from exposure to organophosphate house sprays. Dilute malathion is approved for cat use.

These products can be recognized by reading the label for instructions in case of toxicity. On products containing organophosphates, the drug 2-PAM will be mentioned as an antidote. On products containing carbamates, atropine should be listed as the antidote.

Acute poisoning causes your eyes to blur because your pupils become narrow. You may salivate, tear, wheeze, have muscle cramps, vomit, have diarrhea and feel weak. In severe cases, death occurs from either heart block or from paralysis that leads to suffocation.

There are specific antidotes for this class of insecticide, so medical help should be sought immediately. As with all toxic exposures that occur from topical applications, the animal or person should be washed to prevent any further absorption.

Organophosphates can also cause long-term adverse effects from chronic exposure. Most of the long term negative effects involve loss of nerve function. More subtle effects have included memory loss, decreased alertness, sleep disorders and psychotic reactions.

Dichlorvos and carbaryl are thought to cause cancer. Malathion and chlorpyrifos are suspected of causing birth defects.

Organochlorines

This class of insecticides contains some potentially toxic compounds. However, methoxychlor is the only one commonly used on small animals. Side-effects are uncommon. Depression, weakness and diarrhea have occurred in cases of overdose. Animal studies have suggested that methoxychlor does not cause cancer or birth defects.

Pyrethrins and Synthetic Pyrethroids

Pyrethrins are very commonly employed as on-cat treatments. They are derived from natural products and therefore have a reputation for safety. However, animals can convulse and die from high doses so the products should be used sensibly. Most cases of human toxicity have involved ingestion of these products by small children. Some people can develop a contact dermatitis rash after repeated exposures to pyrethrins. Occasionally, they may cause asthmatic attacks, and rarely they cause severe, potentially deadly allergic reactions known as anaphylaxis. Pyrethrin cross-reacts with ragweed and may be more problematic to people and animals that are allergic to ragweed. Animals that are allergic to pyrethrins may develop hives. This happens after a sensitive animal has been treated repeatedly. True allergic reactions require previous exposure. Thus, although pyrethrins are the safest insecticides, appropriate caution is still advised.

Blockade™ (Hartz Mountain) is a combination of the pyrethroid (a synthetic pyrethrin) fenvalerate and an insect repellent called N,N-diethyl-m-toluamide (DEET). Although the toxicity of each of these ingredients is quite low, there have been problems with the combination. Both cats and dogs have died after being treated with this product. The signs of toxicity include tremors, salivation and death. Respiratory failure caused the deaths. Although these reactions have been rare, the product should be used exactly as recommended by the manufacturer.

Permethrins are another man-made pyrethrin. They are very stable, therefore they last longer. In low concentrations, they may be used on cats. Higher concentrations, which are safe for dogs, may be toxic to cats. Preventic Spray™ (Virbac) is safe, long-lasting and highly effective in dogs. It is toxic to cats.

Piperonyl butoxide (PBO)

Piperonyl butoxide is not an insecticide. It is added to pyrethrin and pyrethroid products to make them work better. It is usually the culprit that causes excessive salivation in cats after flea spray is applied. Long term use may cause neurologic side-effects.

AMITRAZ

Amitraz is most commonly used for treating demodectic mange in dogs. It is also available as a collar to prevent tick attachment. Side-effects are most common in very small dogs as well as cats. The most common side-effects are depression and vomiting. There is also a specific antidote for this toxicity. Amitraz should not be applied by diabetic people or to diabetic animals. It causes your blood sugar to rise. This is only a problem in diabetics. Use amitraz with great caution, if at all, in cats. Be aware that amitraz-

Ocicat diligently grooming itself. Cats are one of the cleanest of household pets. Photo by Isabelle Francais.

containing products are currently not licensed for use on cats.

IVERMECTIN

Ivermectin is used for a wide variety of parasites in small animals. It is usually given orally or by injection under the skin. Ivermectin is not approved for use in cats at all. High doses have been used to treat ear mites in cats. Many practitioners routinely use more than 60 times the approved dose (for heartworm prevention in dogs) to treat a variety of mite infections. Several dog breeds are sensitive to the effects of ivermectin; death from ivermectin has been seen in kittens.

Signs of ivermectin toxicosis are related to the nervous system. Animals may wobble or appear drunk. In severe cases, the animal may become comatose or die. Signs of ivermectin toxicosis may develop in 4 to 12 hours after administration.

I have primarily seen ivermectin toxicosis when owners attempted to use the cattle form of this drug on their pets. The large-animal ivermectins are extremely concentrated, and it is easy to overdose your pet.

ALTERNATIVE METHODS OF FLEA CONTROL

There are many supposedly safe alternatives to parasiticidal products. Garlic, thiamin, sulfur and yeast are fed to pets to prevent fleas. Ultrasonic collars and light traps are touted to drive fleas away or catch them. Some use Avon Skin-So-Soft™ as an insect repellent. These products do not appear to be unsafe, but, unfortunately, they have also never been proven effective in clinical studies. The ingredients in Skin-So-Soft™ are a well-kept industry secret. Therefore, the safety of this product when used on animals for insect control has not been evaluated.

One safe, completely non-toxic method of removing fleas is the use of a flea comb. This very fine-toothed comb has 31 teeth to one inch. This allows fleas to be manually removed. I prefer to use a flea comb on flea infested puppies and kittens. Unfortunately, fleas must be removed before the pet comes in to infest your house. This technique will not adequately protect flea allergic animals that cannot tolerate any flea bites.

METHOD OF APPLICATION

The method of pesticide application is important in determining the overall risk from contact with the product. On-animal products that are packaged to be used as is are generally less toxic than products that must be diluted prior to use. Products that do not require dilution include shampoos, sprays and powders. Dips are the most common form of concentrate. Great care must be taken in measuring so that the proper dilution is obtained. General guidelines would include the wearing of gloves and protective clothing and eyewear while applying dips and sprays. Any skin that contacts the product should be thoroughly washed with soap and water. Dips should be applied in well-ventilated areas. In my practice, we never dip cats. Even products that have been labeled as appropriate for cats have caused deaths. Dogs that are dipped frequently should be thoroughly shampooed prior to dipping. This will eliminate any residual parasiticide still present on the dog from the last dip. Also, bathing prior to dipping allows the dip to penetrate the coat more thoroughly.

Powders are generally less effective than sprays. This may be because the powder does not adhere to fur as well as sprays. It is not uncommon for pets treated with powders to leave small powder spots on furniture and carpets. I prefer formulations that adhere to the pet. Powders may also be irritating to pet owners or animals with breathing problems, especially during application.

Products sold as systemic spot-ons are very concentrated. They should be handled with great care and gloves should be worn. The product must be allowed to completely dry prior to handling the dog. These products are also too toxic for cats. Groomers have become seriously ill from handling a highly concentrated fenthion product.

Sprays are an effective and safe form of delivery. Many animals who object to the sound of the sprayer can be effectively treated by spraying the product on a cloth. The cloth is then rubbed on the animal. A hollow brush that delivers insecticide through holes at the end of the bristles is also an effective way to apply spray to pets that resist being sprayed directly. The product is sold through veterinarians and pet supply houses as a "brushette." A recent study found that cats salivated less when sprays were applied using a "brushette".

Some sprays contain alcohol. They tend to kill fleas extremely fast. Unfortunately, they dry your pets' skin. Also, the alcohol is painful for pets that have scratched until their skin is broken. I do not use alcohol sprays in my practice.

Some clients are disturbed by the impression that fleas are not killed by their choice of flea spray. If you spray a flea directly with a pyrethrin-based flea spray without any alcohol, it does not die immediately. It will, however, die eventually; true resistance is rare. The impression of resistance occurs because of the slower kill time of the newer, less toxic flea products.

More recent developments in products include the formulation of insecticidal "mousse." The insecticide, usually a pyrethrin, is in a formulation similar to hair mousse. Cats who object to the "hiss" of a spray bottle may be especially amenable to this formulation. Ectofoam™ by Virbac is an example of a mousse which is labeled for use even in very young animals.

Flea collars rarely cause toxicity problems. Unfortunately, they are not generally **effective**. Cats have died from organophosphate-impregnated collars. Electronic flea collars have also been demonstrated as ineffective at repelling fleas. In addition, they produce an annoying high-pitched tone that is audible to both dogs and cats although people can't hear it.

However the product is applied, care must be taken around the pet's eyes. Dips or sprays should be sponged on with a cloth instead of applied directly on the face. In years past, we routinely put bland eye ointment in animals' eyes before bathing. I no longer recommend this. If insecticide is splashed in the pet's eye, there is evidence that the ointment causes it to stay in the eye longer. Ointment will also inhibit flushing out the eye. Animals have developed very painful ulcers on the surface of their eyes because of this practice. Should insecticide be splashed in your or your pet's eye, flush it thoroughly with saline solution. This is sold over the counter for contact lens wearers. Medical or veterinary advice should be sought immediately. It is very difficult to determine if the eye has been damaged without special procedures.

Technicians and groomers who dip frequently should be discouraged from wearing contacts at work. There are two reasons for this. First, should they be splashed in the eye, the contact may cause the parasiticide to be retained in the eye. This may cause more damage. Secondly, soft contacts may absorb fumes from concentrated products, even when none of the solution gets directly in the eye. This has been reported to cause eye irritation or damage to the eye's surface.

The method of application is also important in environmental treatments. If the ingredients are identical, sprays are less toxic than foggers.Sprays may be applied directly to problem areas of furniture and carpet. Foggers are disseminated in a fine mist in a perfect circle around the can. Foggers allow insecticide to settle on everything in the room, including your bedding, your children's toys, the table where you eat, and so on. Cooking utensils and surfaces must be covered and cleaned. Additionally, foggers are less effective than the sprays on "flea-friendly" areas such as under beds, corners and closets. This lower efficacy leads to increased exposure as the environment needs to be retreated more often. When either form of environmental insecticide is used, remove all animals from the house. Do not allow children and pets to return until the carpets are thoroughly dried. In my house, after using a spray, this takes about an hour. The actual time depends on how heavy your application is, the temperature and the product used. If foggers are used, vacate the house for 2-3 hours. Then open the windows and allow the house to air out for several hours. In my practice, people with respiratory difficulties, such as asthma, seem to be bothered more by the residual odor of foggers than that of sprays. Check the label prior to using any type of sprayer or fogger. Follow the instructions of the manufacturer. Most of these products are extremely toxic to birds and fish.

SUMMARY

The point of this chapter is not to frighten or discourage use of

Symptoms that require immediate medical attention. Not all signs will be present. If one or more are seen, see your doctor. Excessive salivation in cats is common after applying flea sprays. This may not require veterinary attention if it is the only sign present.

- excess tearing
- difficulty breathing
- blue tint to the gums
- pinpoint pupils
- vomiting or diarrhea
- abdominal cramping

- sweating
- facial twitching
- "sawhorse stance"
- hyperactivity
- weakness
- seizures

insecticides. It is meant to emphasize the real and potential problems with their use. To summarize:

•Always follow the manufacturer's and your veterinarian's instructions. Most toxic reactions are due to applying higher concentrations or more frequent applications than recommended. This is one time where more is definitely not better!

•Be mindful of delayed toxicity as well as acute problems.

•Err on the side of caution. If you think you or your pet may be having a reaction, seek professional medical attention immediately! Take the product with you so your medical professional can see the ingredients.

•Pick products with low toxicities. Be especially careful of using multiple products with the same toxicities. Do not use two organophosphates or carbamates together. Pyrethrins may be safely used with these products.

•Do not use flea control prod-

ucts on sick or pregnant animals. Do not use flea control products on puppies or kittens less than 8 weeks of age without consulting your veterinarian.

•Do not induce vomiting unless instructed to do so. Depressed individuals may drown in their vomit.

•Remember, your veterinarian is trained to help you select the appropriate combination of insecticides for both your home and pets.

ADDITIONAL READING

Bukowski J: Real and potential occupational health risks associated with insecticide use. The Compendium for Continuing Education in *Small Animal Medicine* Vol. 12, No. 11, Nov. 1990, pg. 1617-1623.

Greek J.S. and K.A. Moriello: Treatment of common parasiticidal toxicities in small animals. *Feline Practice* Vol. 19, No. 4, July/August 1991, pg. 11-18.

Greek J.S.: Environmental flea control: General guidelines and recent advances. *Veterinary Medicine*: Aug. 1994, pg. 763-769.

Where to Find Help!

By Lowell Ackerman, DVM, PhD
Diplomate, American College of Veterinary Dermatology
Mesa Veterinary Hospital, Ltd.
858 N. Country Club Drive
Mesa, AZ 85201

INTRODUCTION

When your pet has a skin problem, you have a lot of options these days. Your veterinarian is still the best resource to contact first because he or she can do an initial assessment and decide whether the condition warrants referral to a specialist. Groomers are also important, and are especially useful when a pet has a non-medical problem, such as mats, poor condition of the fur, dandruff, and some external parasites (such as fleas and ticks). Many groomers have also been trained in the safe use of insecticides and can properly and safely apply these preparations to your pet.

Veterinarians and pet paraprofessionals are gaining more and more skills when it comes to recognizing and managing pet skin and haircoat problems. Dermatology is recognized as a specialty discipline by the American Veterinary Medical Association, and board-certified diplomates of the American College of Veterinary Dermatology are entitled to refer to themselves as veterinary dermatologists. Of course, there are many veterinarians with a special interest in dermatology, but the board-certified dermatologists listed in this chapter have completed recognized specialty residency programs and passed the stringent examinations of the American College of Veterinary Dermatology.

The grooming situation is also not static. At present, there aren't too many restrictions on who can call themselves a groomer, and so talents and training are quite variable. In some states, groomers must pass examinations on the safe use of insecticides, but this is not true everywhere. Groomers are in the process of trying to regulate themselves, and this will help the public determine who has appropriate credentials and who doesn't. At the end of this chapter, Hazel Christiansen of the American Grooming Shop Association shares her views on the current status of "The Professional Groomer".

VETERINARY DERMATOLOGY

The American College of Veterinary Dermatology (ACVD) is an official specialty board organization, accredited by the American Veterinary Medical Association and charged with maintenance of high standards of postgraduate training in veterinary dermatology. The ACVD is empowered to examine qualifying candidates and confer Diplomate status in the College. Board certification in the ACVD has been achieved by 82 veterinarians in the United States, Canada, and Australia since its creation in 1978. An updated directory of board-certified veterinarians is provided in this chapter.

The ACVD's functions are diverse, ranging from regulation of residency training programs in veterinary dermatology and conferring of Diplomate status to active participation in continuing education, to an annual meeting, and scientific program, and funding of research grants.

The ACVD established criteria for approval of residency programs to maintain high standards of training. Most dermatology residency programs are conducted at veterinary schools. However, alternative residency programs are available, whereby trainees gain the bulk of their required practice experience working under an ACVD Diplomate in private practice.

One of the major functions of the College is to grant diplomate status to trained veterinary dermatologists. The process of board certification begins with the applicant's submission of credentials; verification of

training in an approved program, scientific publications, letters of evaluation, and written case reports. Each applicant's credentials are reviewed carefully. If accepted, the applicant become eligible to take the certification examination.

The College co-sponsors a four-day scientific program held each spring. The annual meeting is an opportunity for presentation of pre-publication research studies and case reports, as well as review sessions and guest speakers addressing a variety of topics in dermatology.

The ACVD sponsors several programs to disseminate knowledge and improve the level of training of general veterinary practitioners in dermatology. General practitioner-level review courses are offered at the annual meeting. The ACVD is co-sponsor of the World Congress on Veterinary Dermatology held every three years. The last meeting was held in Edinburgh, Scotland in September, 1996.

A limited number of research grants are offered by the ACVD annually on a competitive proposal basis. Many of these grants have been used to fund research activities that lead to new diagnostic procedures and treatments for your pet's skin problems. The majority of the research sponsorship is from drug companies. However, you, too, can help by making a donation to the ACVD Research Fund.

Your donation, or a donation made by your veterinarian in the name of your pet, will be placed into a large research pool. Members of the ACVD Research Committee will decide what research projects should be funded that will promote advancement in the field of veterinary dermatology.

The ACVD is a non-profit organization and your cash donation will be tax deductible. A letter commending and identifying you as a sponsor will also be forwarded in response to all donations. Checks should be made payable to ACVD Research Funding Program and mailed to Dr. Wayne Rosenkrantz, ACVD Chairman, Research Funding Committee, 13132 Garden Grove Blvd., Suite B, Garden Grove, CA 92643.

ACVD DIPLOMATES
(as of July, 1996)
(Compiled by Lowell Ackerman, DVM, ACVD)

Ackerman, Lowell
  Arizona, Scottsdale
  Arizona, Mesa
  Ontario, Thornhill
Anderson, Richard
  Massachusetts, Boston
Angarano, Donna
  Alabama, Auburn
Atlee, Barbara
  North Carolina, Raleigh
Austin, Victor
  California, Westlake Village
Baker, Benjamin
  Washington, Pullman
Barbet, Joy
  Florida, Archer
Beale, Karin
  Texas, Houston
  Texas, San Antonio
Bevier, Diane
  North Carolina, Raleigh
Blakemore, James
  Indiana, West Lafayette
Breen, Patrick
  Kentucky, Louisville

  Ohio, Cincinatti
  Ohio, Columbus
  Ohio, Richfield Village
Brignac, Michele
  Florida, Ft. Walton Beach
Buerger, Robert
  Maryland, Baltimore
Byre, Kevin
  Illinois, Urbana
Caciolo, Paul
  Missouri, St. Louis
Campbell, Karen
  Illinois, Urbana
Cayette, Suzanne
  Florida, Largo
Chalmers, Stephanie
  California, Santa Rosa
  California, Walnut Creek
Charach, Mike
  British Columbia, Coquitlam
  British Columbia, Kelowna
  British Columbia, Nanaimo
  British Columbia, Richmond
  British Columbia, Victoria
Chester, David
  Texas, College Station
Conroy, James (Pathologist)
  Arizona, Prescott
DeBoer, Douglas
  Wisconsin, Madison
Delger, Julie
  South Carolina, Columbia
Doering, George
  California, Walnut Creek
Donnelly, Cynthia
  Arizona, Tucson
Duclos, David
  Washington, Lynnwood
Evans, Anne
  Massachusetts, North Grafton
Fadok, Valerie
  Colorado, Denver
Foil, Carol
  Louisiana, Baton Rouge
Frank, Linda
  Tennessee, Knoxville

Garfield, Reid
  Oklahoma, Tulsa
  Texas, Dallas
  Texas, Ft. Worth
  Texas, Tyler
Gilbert, Patricia
  California, Rancho Santa Fe
Globus, Helen
  Minnesota, Apple Valley
  Minnesota, Golden Valley
Gordon, John
  Ohio, Columbus
Gram, Dunbar
  Virginia, Virginia Beach
  Virginia, Richmond
Greek, Jean
  Kansas, Overland Park
Griffin, Craig
  Alaska, Anchorage
  Alaska, Fairbanks
  California, Alta Loma
  California, Bakersfield
  California, Garden Grove
  California, Los Gatos
  California, San Diego
  California, Scotts Valley
  Hawaii, Honolulu
  Hawaii, Kamuela
  Hawaii, Kaneohe
  Hawaii, Kona
  Hawaii, Wahiawa
  Hawaii, Waipahu
  Nevada, Las Vegas
Hall, Jan
  Quebec, Ville Saint-Laurent
Halliwell, Richard
  Scotland, Edinburgh
Hansen, Bruce
  Virginia, Springfield
Hillier, Andrew
  Ohio, Columbus
Ihrke, Peter
  California, Davis
Jeffers, James
  Maryland, Gaithersburg
Jeromin, Alice

  Ohio, Brecksville
  Ohio, Toledo
  Pennsylvania, Wexford
Kalaher, Kathleen
  Maryland, Baltimore
Kirk, Robert W.
  New York, Ithaca
Kuhl, Karen
  Illinois, Riverwoods
Kunkle, Gail
  Florida, Gainesville
Kwochka, Kenneth
  Ohio, Columbus
LeMarie, Stephen L.
  Louisiana, Baton Rouge
Lewis, Diane
  Florida, Gainesville
Lewis, Thomas
  Arizona, Mesa
  Arizona, Tucson
  New Mexico, Albuquerque
  New Mexico, Santa Teresa
  Utah, Salt Lake City
Logas, Dawn
  Florida, Gainesville
MacDonald, John
  Alabama, Auburn
Manning, Thomas
  North Carolina, Raleigh
McKeever, Patrick
  Minnesota, St. Paul
Medleau, Linda
  Georgia, Athens
Merchant, Sandra
  Louisiana, Baton Rouge
Messinger, Linda
  Colorado, Denver
Miller, Wiilliam
  New York, Ithaca
Moriello, Karen
  Wisconsin, Madison
Mueller, Ralf
  Australia, Victoria
Muller, George
  California, Walnut Creek
Mundell, Alan

Washington, Seattle
Nesbitt, Gene
Maine, Standish
New Jersey, West Caldwell
New York, Coram
Olivry, Thierry
North Carolina, Raleigh
Panic, Rada
New Jersey, Tinton Falls
New York, Burnt Hills
New York, Mineola
Paradis, Manon
Quebec, St. Hyacinthe
Phillips, Margaret
Tennesse, Nashville
Plant, Jon
California, Santa Monica
California, Ventura
California, Woodland Hills
Power, Helen
California, Los Gatos
Pucheu-Haston, Cherie
North Carolina, Durham
Rachofsky, Marc
Texas, Dallas
Reedy, Lloyd
Texas, Dallas
Texas, Fort Worth
Texas, Plano
Texas, Tyler
Reinke, Susan
California, Corte Madera
Helton-Rhodes, Karen
New York, Floral Park
Rosenkrantz, Wayne S.
Alaska, Anchorage
Alaska, Fairbanks
California, Alta Loma
California, Bakersfield
California, Garden Grove
California, Los Gatos
California, San Diego
California, Scotts Valley
Hawaii, Honolulu
Hawaii, Kamuela

Hawaii, Kaneohe
Hawaii, Kona
Hawaii, Wahiawa
Hawaii, Waipahu
Nevada, Las Vegas
Rosser, Edmund
Michigan, East Lansing
Scheidt, Vicki
New Hampshire, Lyme
Schick, Robert
Georgia, Augusta
Georgia, Riverdale
Georgia, Roswell
Schmeitzel, Lynn
Tennessee, Knoxville
Schwartzman, Robert
Pennsylvania, Philadelphia
Scott, Danny
New York, Ithaca
Shanley, Kevin
Deleware, Newark
Pennsylvania, Valley Forge
Shoulberg, Nina
New York, Katonah
New York, Yonkers
Small, Erwin
Illinois, Urbana
Sousa, Candace
California, Sacramento
Stannard, Anthony (Pathologist)
California, Davis
Stewart, Laurie
Massachusetts, Acton
Torres, Sheila
Minnesota, St. Paul
Werner, Alexander
California, Camarillo
California, Los Angeles
California, Studio City
Nevada, Reno
White, Patricia
Georgia, Avondale
Georgia, Marietta
White, Stephen
Colorado, Fort Collins

Locations of Veterinary Dermatology Referral Centers

Compiled by: Lowell Ackerman, DVM, Diplomate, ACVD

ALASKA
Northern Lights Animal Clinic
Dr. Craig Griffin
Dr. Wayne Rosenkrantz
2002 W. Benson
Anchorage, AK 99517
(907) 276-2340
(Visits twice yearly)

Aurora Animal Clinic
Dr. Craig Griffin
Dr. Wayne Rosenkrantz
1651 College Rd.
Fairbanks, AK 99507
(907) 452-6055
(Visits approximately twice yearly)

ALABAMA
Auburn University
Dr. Donna Walton Angarano
College of Veterinary Medicine
Auburn, AL 36849
(205) 844-4690

Auburn University
Dr. John M. Macdonald
College of Veterinary Medicine
Auburn, AL 36849
(205) 844-4000

ARIZONA
Mesa Veterinary Hospital, Ltd.
Dr. Lowell J. Ackerman
858 N. Country Club Drive
Mesa, AZ 85201
(602) 833-7330

Mesa Veterinary Hospital, Ltd
Dr. Thomas P. Lewis II
858 N. Country Club Drive
Mesa, AZ 85201
(602) 833-7330

Southwest Veterinary Specialist
Dr. Thomas P. Lewis II
141 East Ft. Lowell Road
Tucson, AZ 85705
(602) 888-4498

Dr. Cynthia Donnelly
2602 E. Avenida de Posada
Tucson, AZ 85718
(520) 327-5624

CALIFORNIA
Animal Dermatology Center
Dr. Stephanie A. Chalmers
4900 Sonoma Hwy.
Santa Rosa, CA 95409
(707) 538-4643

Veterinary Dermatology Service
Dr. Stephanie A. Chalmers
1411 Treat Blvd.
Walnut Creek, CA 94596
(510) 934-8051

Veterinary Dermatology Service
Dr. George G. Doering
1411 Treat Blvd.
Walnut Creek, CA 94596

(510) 934-8051

Veterinary Specialty Hospital
Dr. Patricia Gilbert
6525 Calle Del Nido, Box 9727
Rancho Santa Fe, CA 92067
(619) 759-1777

Animal Dermatology Clinic
Dr. Craig Griffin
Dr. Wayne Rosenkrantz
13132 Garden Grove Blvd.
Garden Grove, CA 92643
(714) 971-6211

Animal Dermatology Clinic
Dr. Craig Griffin
Dr. Wayne Rosenkrantz
13240 Evening Creek Drive, #302
San Diego, CA 92128
(619) 486-4600

Baseline Animal Hospital
Dr. Craig Griffin
Dr. Wayne Rosenkrantz
9350 Baseline Rd., Suite A
Alta Loma, CA 91701
(714) 486-4600
(Monthly visits)

Valley Oak Veterinary Clinic
Dr. Craig Griffin
Dr. Wayne Rosenkrantz
4650 Scotts Valley Drive

Scotts Valley, CA 95060
(408) 438-6546
(Visits approximately
   twice yearly)

Oak Meadow Veterinary
   Hospital
Dr. Craig Griffin
Dr. Wayne Rosenkrantz
641 University Avenue
Los Gatos, CA 95030
(408) 354-0838
(Visits approximately
   twice yearly)

Bakersfield Veterinary
   Clinic
Dr. Craig Griffin
Dr. Wayne Rosenkrantz
4410 Wible Rd.
Bakersfield, CA 93313
(805) 834-6005
(Visits approximately
   twice yearly)

University of California
Dr. Peter Ihrke
School of Veterinary
   Medicine
Department of Medicine
Davis, Ca 95616
(916) 752-1355

Animal Dermatology
   Specialty Clinic
Dr. Jon D. Plant
1304 Wilshire Blvd.
Santa Monica, CA 90403
(310) 394-6982

Animal Dermatology
   Specialty Clinic
Dr. Jon D. Plant
23015 S. Victoria Ave.
Ventura, CA 93003
(310) 394-6982
(800) 606-ADSC

Animal Dermatology
   Specialty Clinic

Dr. Jon D. Plant
20037 Ventura Blvd.,
   Suite 105
Woodland Hills, CA
   91364
(310) 394-6982
(800) 606-ADSC

Dermatology for Animals
Dr. Helen T. Power
17480 Shelburne Way
Los Gatos, CA 95030
(408) 354-1840

Madera Pet Hospital
Dr. Susan I. Reinke
5796 Paradise Drive
Corte Madera, CA 94925
(415) 924-1271

Animal Dermatology
   Clinic
Dr. Candace Sousa
5701 H Street
Sacramento, CA 95819
(916) 451-6445

University of California
Dr. Anthony Stannard
School of Veterinary
   Medicine
Department of Medicine
Davis, CA 95616
(916) 752-1363

Valley Veterinary
   Specialty Services
Dr. Alexander Werner
Animal Dermatology
   Centers
13125 Ventura Blvd.
Studio City, CA 91604
(818) 981-8877
(800) 781-8877

Animal Dermatology
   Centers
Dr. Alexander Werner
1221-B Avenida Acaso
Camarillo, CA 93012

(818) 981-8877

Animal Dermatology
   Centers
Dr. Alexander Werner
4254 Eagle Rock Blvd.
Los Angeles, CA 90065
(818) 981-8877

Animal Dermatology
   Centers
Dr. Alexander Werner
1736 S. Sepulveda Blvd.,
   Ste C
Los Angeles, CA 90025
(818) 981-8877

COLORADO
Dr. Linda M. Messinger
Veterinary Referral
   Center, Colorado
2401 South Downing
Denver, CO 80210
(303) 733-2440

Colorado State University
Dr. Stephen D. White
College of Veterinary
   Medicine
Dept. of Clinical Studies
Fort Collins, CO 80523
(303) 221-4535

DELAWARE
Newark Animal Hospital
Dr. Kevin J. Shanley
245 E. Cleveland Avenue
Newark, DE 19711
(302) 737-8100
(800) 394-3874

FLORIDA
Friendship Veterinary
   Clinic
Dr. Michele Brignac
623 Beal Parkway
Ft. Walton Beach, FL
   32548
(904) 862-9813

Tampa Bay Veterinary
    Referral
Dr. Suzanne M. Cayatte
1501-A Belcher Road
    South
Largo, FL 34641
(813) 539-7990

University of Florida
Dr. Gail A. Kunkle
Dr. Diane T. Lewis
Dr. Dawn Logas
College of Veterinary
    Medicine
Box 100126
Gainesville, FL 32610-
    0126
(904) 392-4700

GEORGIA
University of Georgia
Dr. Linda Medleau
College of Veterinary
    Medicine
Department of Small
    Animal Medicine
Athens, GA 30602
(706) 542-3221

Atlanta Animal Allergy
    and Dermatology
Dr. Robert O. Schick
280 S. Atlanta Street
Roswell, GA 30075
(404) 642-9800

Atlanta Animal Allergy
    and Dermatology
Dr. Robert O. Schick
6607 Powers Street
Riverdale, GA 30274
(404) 642-9800

Atlanta Animal Allergy
    and Dermatology
Dr. Robert O. Schick
Animal Emergency Clinic
    of Augusta
2401-B Washington
    Road

Augusta, GA 30904
(404) 642-9800

Atlanta Veterinary Skin
    and Allergy Clinic
Dr. Patricia D. White
33 Avondale Plaza North
Avondale Estates, GA
    30002
(404) 294-0580

Atlanta Veterinary Skin
    and Allergy Clinic
Dr. Patricia D. White
828 Cobb Parkway
Marietta, GA 30062
(404) 294-0580

HAWAII
Aloha Animal Hospital
    Associates
Dr. Craig Griffin
Dr. Wayne Rosenkrantz
4224 Wailae Avenue
Honolulu, HI 96816
(808) 734-2242
(Visits approximately
    twice yearly)

Animal Clinic Waipahu
Dr. Craig Griffin
Dr. Wayne Rosenkrantz
94-806 Moloalo Street
Waipahu, HI 96797
(808) 671-1751
(Visits approximately
    twice yearly)

Honolulu Pet Clinic
Dr. Craig Griffin
Dr. Wayne Rosenkrantz
1115 Young Street
Honolulu, HI 96814
(808) 537-5336
(Visits approximately
    twice yearly)

Kaneohe Veterinary
    Clinic
Dr. Craig Griffin

Dr. Wayne Rosenkrantz
45-480 Kaneohe Bay
    Drive
Kaneohe, HI 96744
(808) 235-3634
(Visits approximately
    twice yearly)

Kilani Pet Clinic
Dr. Craig Griffin
Dr. Wayne Rosenkrantz
810 Kilani Avenue
Wahiawa, HI 96786
(808) 622-2607
(Visits approximately
    twice yearly)

Kona Coast Veterinary
    Hospital
Dr. Craig Griffin
Dr. Wayne Rosenkrantz
P.O. Box 730
Kealakekua
Kona, HI 96750
(808) 322-3469
(Visits approximately
    twice yearly)

Veterinary Associates
Dr. Craig Griffin
Dr. Wayne Rosenkrantz
P.O. Box 839
Kamuela, HI 96743
(808) 885-7941
(Visits approximately
    twice yearly)

ILLINOIS
Dr. Kevin Byre
Small Animal Clinic
University of Illinois
1008 W. Hazelwood
Urbana, IL 61801
(217) 333-6868

University of Illinois
Dr. Karen L. Campbell
Dept. of Veterinary
    Clinical Medicine
1008 West Hazelwood Dr.

Urbana, IL 61801
(217) 333-5300
Dermatology Referral
  Service
Dr. Karen A. Kuhl
Veterinary Specialty
  Clinic
2551 Warrenville Road
Downers Grove, IL 60515
708-934-6056

INDIANA
Purdue University
Dr. James C. Blakemore
School of Veterinary
  Medicine
Lynn Hall 1248
West Lafayette, IN
  47907-1248
(317) 494-1107

KANSAS
Dermatology and Allergy
  Clinic
Dr. Jean S. Greek
10333 Metcalf Avenue
Overland Park, KS 66212
(913) 381-3937

KENTUCKY
Louisville Veterinary
  Dermatology Services
Dr. Patrick T. Breen
10466 Shelbyville Road
Louisville, KY 40223
(502) 245-7863

LOUISIANA
Veterinary Teaching
  Hospital and Clinics
Dr. Carol S. Foil
Dr. Sandra R. Merchant
Louisiana State
  University
Baton Rouge, LA 70803
(504) 346-3333

Dr. Stephen L. LeMarie
Companion Animal
  Dermatology Referral

Services
12531 Coursey Blvd.,
  #2102
Baton Rouge, LA 70816
(504) 751-7763

MAINE
Animal Dermatology
  Consultants (Mobile)
Dr. Gene H. Nesbitt
42 Highland Road (mail only)
Standish, ME 04084
(207) 893-0058

MARYLAND
Veterinary Dermatology
  Center
Dr. Robert G. Buerger
32 Mellor Avenue
Baltimore, MD 21228
(410) 788-8130

Dr. James Jeffers
9039 Gaither Rd.
Gaithersburg, MD 20877
(301) 977-9169

MASSACHUSETTS
Angell Memorial Animal
  Hospital
Dr. Richard K. Anderson
350 South Huntington
  Avenue
Boston, MA 02130
(617) 522-7282

Tufts University
Dr. Laurie J. Stewart
School of Veterinary
  Medicine
200 Westboro Rd.
Acton, MA 01536
(508) 839-5302

MICHIGAN
Michigan State
  University
Dr. Edmund J. Rosser, Jr.
Dept. of Small Animal
  Clinical Studies

Veterinary Medical
  Center D-208
East lansing, MI 48824-
  1314
(517) 355-7721

MINNESOTA
Veterinary Dermatology
  Service
Dr. Helen Globus
South Metro Animal
  Emergency Care
14520 Pennock Avenue
Apple Valley, MN 55124
(612) 928-8097

Veterinary Dermatology
  Service
Dr. Helen Globus
Affiliated Emergency
  Veterinary Services
4708 Olson Memorial
  Highway
Golden Valley, MN 55422
(612) 928-8097

University of Minnesota
Dr. Patrick J. McKeever
Dr. Sheila Torres
Dept. of Small Animal
  Clinical Sciences
1352 Boyd Avenue
St. Paul, MN 55108
(612) 625-9229

MISSOURI
The Animal Skin Clinic
Dr. Paul Caciolo
11148 Olive Blvd.
St. Louis, MO 63141
(314) 997-0920

NEVADA
Tropicana Veterinary
  Clinic
Dr. Craig Griffin
Dr. Wayne Rosencrantz
2385 E. Tropicana
Las Vegas, NV 89109
(702) 736-4944

(Monthly Visits)

Animal Dermatology
   Centers
Dr. Alexander Werner
855 E. Peckham Lane
Reno, NV 89502
(818) 981-8877

NEW HAMPSHIRE
Animal Dermatology
   Service
Dr. Vicki J. Scheidt
6 Montview Drive
Lyme, NH 03768
(603) 448-3534

NEW JERSEY
West Caldwell Animal
   Hospital
Dr. Gene H. Nesbitt
706 Bloomfield Avenue
West Caldwell, NJ 07006
(201) 226-3727

Garden State Veterinary
   Specialists
Dr. Rada Panic
1 Pine Street
Tinton Falls, NJ 07753
(908) 922-0011

NEW MEXICO
Dermatology Clinic for
   Animals
Dr. Thomas P. Lewis II
Albuquerque Animal
   Emergency Clinic
50055 Prospect Avenue
   NE
Albuquerque, NM 87110
(505) 881-7205

El Abrigado Animal
   Clinic
Dr. Thomas P. Lewis II
900 Country Club Road
Santa Teresa, NM 88008
(505) 589-1818

NEW YORK
Cardiopet
Dr. Karen Helton Rhodes
51 Atlanta Avenue
Floral Park, NY 11001
((800) 726-1212

Cornell University
Dr. William H. Miller, Jr.
College of Veterinary
   Medicine
Department of Clinical
   Sciences
Ithaca, NY 14853
(607) 253-3029

Animal Emergency
   Service
Dr. Gene H. Nesbitt
485 Middle Country Rd.
Coram, NY 11727
(516) 698-2225

Burnt Hills Veterinary
   Hospital
Dr. Rada Panic
145 Goode Street
Burnt Hills, NY 12027
(518) 399-5213

Veterinary Dermatology
   Consulting Service
Dr. Rada Panic
UltraVet Diagnostics
220 E. Jericho Turnpike
Mineola, NY 11501
(516) 294-6680

Cornell University
Dr. Danny W. Scott
College of Veterinary
   Medicine
Department of Clinical
   Sciences
Ithaca, NY 14853
(607) 253-3029

Katonah Veterinary
   Group
Dr. Nina Shoulberg

120 Bedford Road
Katonah, New York
   10536
(914) 232-1800

County Animal Clinic
Dr. Nina Shoulberg
1574 Central Park
   Avenue
Yonkers, New York
   10710
(914) 779-5000

NORTH CAROLINA
Dr. Barbara Atlee
Animal Dermatology &
   Allergy Clinic
1204 Deboy Street
Raleigh, NC 27606-1718
(919) 233-1787

North Carolina State
   University
Dr. Diane E. Bevier
College of Veterinary
   Medicine
4700 Hillsborough Street
Raleigh, NC 27606
(919) 829-4495

North Carolina State
   University
Dr. Thomas O. Manning
College of Veterinary
   Medicine
4700 Hillsborough Street
Raleigh, NC 27606
(919) 821-9500

Dr. Thierry Olivry
North Carolina State
   University
College of Veterinary
   Medicine
4700 Hillsborough Street
Raleigh, NC 27606

Dr. Cheri Pucheu-Haston
2230 Glover Road
Durham, NC 27703

(919) 821-9500

OHIO
Veterinary Dermatology
  Services
Dr. Patrick T. Breen
4725 Cornell Road
Cincinnati, OH 45241
(513) 489-46444
(800) 476-9461

Cleveland Veterinary
  Dermatology Services
Dr. Patrick T. Breen
4050 Broadview Road
Richfield Village, OH
  44286
(216) 659-4169

Columbus Veterinary
  Dermatology Services
Dr. Patrick T. Breen
5747 Cleveland Avenue
Columbus, OH 43231
(614) 891-2070

Med Vet
Dr. John G. Gordon
5747 Cleveland Avenue
Columbus, OH 43231
(614) 891-2070

Veterinary Allergy &
  Dermatology Inc.
Dr. Alice Jeromin
8979 Brecksville Rd.
Brecksville, OH 44141
(216) 278-2446

Veterinary Allergy &
  Dermatology, Inc.
Dr. Alice Jeromin
2785 W. Central Avenue
Toledo, OH 43606
(419) 473-0328

The Ohio State
  University
Dr. Andrew Hillier
Dr. Kenneth W. Kwochka

Dept. of Veterinary
  Clinical Sciences
601 Vernon L. Tharp St.
Columbus, OH 43210
(614) 292-3551

OKLAHOMA
Animal Emergency
  Center
Dr. Reid A. Garfield
Dr. Lloyd M. Reedy
7220 E. 41st.
Tulsa, OK 74145-4504
(214) 241-6266

PENNSYLVANIA
Veterinary Allergy &
  Dermatology, Inc.
Dr. Alice Jeromin
10309 Perry Hwy.
Wexford, PA 15090
(412) 935-5912

Metropolitan Veterinary
  Associates
Dr. Kevin J. Shanley
Box 881, 915 Trooper
  Road
Valley Forge, PA 19482
(610) 650-0747
(610) 666-1050

SOUTH CAROLINA
South Carolina
  Dermatology Referral
  Service
Dr. Julie M. Delger
124 Stonemark Lane
Columbia, SC 29210
(803) 798-0803

TENNESSEE
The University of
  Tennessee
Dr. Linda A. Frank
College of Veterinary
  Medicine
Department of Urban
  Practice
P.O. Box 1071

Knoxville, TN 37901-
  1071
(615) 974-8387

Animal Allergy and
  Dermatology Referral
  Service
Dr. Margaret K. Phillips
5814 Nolensville Rd.,
  Suite 107
Nashville, TN 37211-
  6521
(615) 831-2898

The University of
  Tennessee
Dr. Lynn P. Schmeitzel
College of Veterinary
  Medicine
Department of Urban
  Practice
P.O. Box 1071
Knoxville, TN 37901-
  1071
(615) 974-8387

TEXAS
Gulf Coast Veterinary
  Specialists
Dr. Karin Beale
5255 Beechnut
Houston, TX 77096
(713) 666-4414

Lincoln Heights Animal
  Hospital
Dr. Karin Beale
7510 Broadway
San Antonio, TX 78209
(210) 826-6100

Texas A&M University
Dr. David K. Chester
Dept. of Small Animal
  Medicine and Surgery
College of Veterinary
  Medicine
College Station, TX
  77843
(409) 845-2351

Allergy & Dermatology
   Clinic for Animals
Dr. Marc A. Rachofsky
12101 Greenville
   Avenue, #120
Dallas, TX 75243
(214) 680-0408

Animal Dermatology
   Referral Clinic
Dr. Reid A. Garfield
Dr. Lloyd M. Reedy
2353 Royal Lane
Dallas, TX 75229
(214) 241-6266

Western Hills Animal
   Hospital
Dr. Reid A. Garfield
Dr. Lloyd M. Reedy
3325 Phoenix
Fort Worth, TX 76116
(214) 241-6266

Emergency Clinic of
   Collin County
Dr. Reid A. Garfield
Dr. Lloyd M. Reedy
909 Spring Creek Pkwy.,
   Suite 410
Cross Creek Shopping
   Center
Plano, TX 75074
(214) 241-6266

Emergency Clinic
Dr. Lloyd M. Reedy
Dr. Reid A. Garfield
3326 South S.W. Loop
   323
Tyler, TX 75701
(214) 241-6266

UTAH
Eye Clinic for Animals
Dr. Thomas P. Lewis II
1892 E. Ft. Union Blvd.
Salt Lake City, UT 84121
(801) 942-3937

VIRGINIA
Animal Allergy &
   Dermatology
Dr. Dunbar Gram
3312 West Cary St.
Richmond, VA 23221
(804) 358-3376

Animal Allergy &
   Dermatology
Dr. Dunbar Gram
P.O. Box 6858
Virginia Beach, VA
   23450
(804) 467-3376

Dermatology and Allergy
   Services for Animals
Dr. Bruce L. Hansen
6651-F Backlick Rd.
Springfield, VA 22150
(703) 440-9206

WASHINGTON
Washington State
   University
Dr. Benjamin B. Baker
College of Veterinary
   Medicine
106 McCoy Hall
Pullman, WA 99163
(509) 335-0711

Animal Skin and Allergy
   Clinic
Dr. David D. Duclos
16418 7th Place West
Lynnwood, WA 98037
(206) 742-0342

Animal Dermatology
   Service
Dr. Alan C. Mundell
6525 15th Avenue NW
Seattle, WA 98117
(206) 789-2959

WISCONSIN
University of Wisconsin-

Madison
Dr. Douglas J. Deboer
School of Veterinary
   Medicine
2015 Linden Drive West
Madison, WI 53706
(608) 263-8399

University of Wisconsin-
   Madison
Dr. Karen A. Moriello
School of Veterinary
   Medicine
2015 Linden Drive West
Madison, WI 53706
(608) 263-7600

AUSTRALIA
Animal Skin & Allergy
   Clinic
Dr. Ralf S. Mueller
37 Blackburn Rd.
Mount Waverly, VIC
   3149
Australia
61-3-9887-8844

CANADA
Doncaster Animal Clinic
Dr. Lowell J. Ackerman
99 Henderson Avenue
Thornhill, Ontario
L3T 2K9
(905) 881-2922

Garden City Veterinary
   Hospital
Dr. Michael Charach
140-8040 Garden City
   Road
Richmond, British
   Columbia V6X 2N9
(604) 270-6199

Fairfield Animal Hospital
Dr. Michael Charach
1987 Kirschner Road
Kelowna, British
   Columbia V1Y 4N7

(800) 3337-6838

Island Veterinary
    Hospital
Dr. Michael Charach
1621 Townsite Road
Nanaimo, British
    Columbia V9S 1N3
(800) 337-6838

Central Victoria
    Veterinary Hospital
Dr. Michael Charach
760 Roderick Street
Victoria, British
    Columbia V8X 2R3
(800) 337-6838

After Hours Pet Hospital
Dr. Michael Charach
963 Brunette Avenue
Coquitlam, British
    Columbia V3K 1E1
(604) 270-6199

Dr. Jan A. Hall
Centre Veterinaire
5959 Transcanadienne
Ville Saint-Laurent
Quebec HrT 1A1
(514) 855-5555

Universite de Montreal
Dr. Manon Paradis

Faculte Medicine
    Veterinaire
CP5000
St. Hyacinthe, Quebec
J2S 7C6
(514) 773-0162

GREAT BRITAIN
Royal School of
    Veterinary Studies
Dr. Richard E.W.
    Halliwell
Dept. of Veterinary
    Clinical Studies
Summerhall, Edinburgh
EH3 91Q Scotland
(44) 31 650 6149

Hazel Christiansen has shown dogs in both conformation and obedience in the United States, Canada and Hong Kong. She is President of the American Grooming Shop Association, a national non-profit association, and has been grooming for 30 years. Hazel teaches pet education in the public school system, is a regular on local radio programs, and serves on the editorial board of Casamount Publications. She owns Blue Ribbon Pet Grooming in Lewiston, Idaho.

The Professional Groomer

By Hazel Christiansen
Lewiston, Idaho
President, American Grooming Shop Association
4575 Galley Road, Suite 400A
Colorado Springs, CO 80915

Although there are a lot of groomers out there, training and level of skill are not uniform. Some individuals refer to themselves as dog groomers, some as canine cosmetologists, and others as professional pet stylists. The profession is embarking on a course to provide testing procedures, training seminars, and networking for groomers and would-be groomers.

The International Society of Canine Cosmetologists has a three-stage program of advanced instruction and testing. It provides a validation process for qualified individuals. Level One is called DermaTech. It covers topical skin treatments, chemicals, ergonomics, and breed identification. Level Two, the Certified Master Pet Stylist, includes grooming Non-Sporting, Sporting, and Terrier breeds. After two years of pet styling experience, testing is available for the Master Canine Cosmetologist program. Contact Pam Lauritzen & Co. at 2702 Covington Drive, Garland, TX 75040.

National Dog Groomers Association conducts testing and training seminars. Their testing format requires both written and hands-on grooming to be judged by a panel of judges. Individuals take a written test for Sporting, Non-Sporting, Terriers, and a final exam for National Certified Master Groomer. Contact Jeff Reynolds, National Dog Groomers Association of America, Inc., P.O. Box 101, Clark, PA 16113.

Western World Pet Supply Association conducts training and testing for certification as a Companion Animal Hygienist. The course includes lectures and tapes covering theory. Those who complete all three sections of their course can receive certificates for CAH, Clipper and Scissor Technique, and The Grooming of Cats. Contact Western World Pet Supply Association, Inc. 818-447-2222.

The American Grooming Shop Association is a national non-profit trade association of shop owners and managers. It provides free consultation to its members for solving their business problems. Their educational programs are being formed to allow testing for the individual, and accreditation for the shop itself. AGSA also conducts two seminars per year on "buying, building and operating a successful grooming shop." These seminars cover location, design, business practices, hiring and firing safely, new shop equipment, and other subjects relevant to shop management and ownership. Contact AGSA at 4575 Galley Road, Suite 400-A, Colorado Springs, CO 80915.

International Professional Groomers also have a testing process that includes hands-on grooming and theory. It is a non-profit trade association. They test a groomer's technique on a dog from Sporting, Non-Sporting and Terrier Groups, and have a Master's test as well. They can be contacted at 1108 Elk Grove, IL 60007.

State organizations for groomers are active in Illinois, California, Washington and others. While they may not have testing procedures, they do conduct grooming seminars.

Grooming seminars are held throughout the United States. These seminars often include breed demonstrations, suggestions on ways to increase client satisfaction and how to run a grooming business more efficiently. Some of the major seminars are:

- Atlanta Pet Fair, 4782 Jimmy Carter Blvd., Ste 2a, Norcross, GA 30093. (404) 925-9284.
- All-American Midwest Dog Grooming Seminar. Jerry Schinberg, (708) 364-4547.

- Groom Expo, Barkleigh Publications, 6 State Road, #113, Mechanicsburg, PA 17055.
- Intergroom, 250 E. 73rd St., Ste 4F, New York, NY, 10021 ATTN: Shirlee Kalstone (212) 628-3537.

Many trade shows and grooming seminars also have grooming contests, where pet stylists can have the opportunity to demonstrate their work. The dogs are groomed in front of the crowd, then a judge checks the work and awards prizes for the best-groomed dogs. There are different classes available, depending upon the breed of dog and the groomer's experience.

There are also contests for creative grooming, where the contestant thinks of a theme, grooms the dog to fit the theme, then decorates around the dog. Sometimes these contestants complete the image with music. It allows the creative and artistic ability of the individual to shine. Groomers usually pay an entrance fee, and cash awards are usually given as prizes.

Groomers winning the most points at shows across the U.S. may be selected for "Groom Team," and have an opportunity to represent their country in international competition.

INDEX

Page numbers in **boldface** refer to illustrations.